THE WEST HIGHLAND RAILWAY:
120 Years

John McGregor

AMBERLEY

Acknowledgements

Further thanks are owed to all whose assistance and support saw my two Through Time books to completion in 2013 and then sustained this new venture. I'm grateful to Louis Archard of Amberley Publishing for suggesting that the West Highland's 120th anniversary should not pass unnoticed.

Photographs and Other Supporting Materials

John Alsop Collection; Casserley Collection (H. C. & R. M. Casserley); Alex Gillespie Collection; Glenfinnan Station Museum Trust Archive; Robert Grieves Collection, courtesy John Sinclair; Hennigan Collection, courtesy W. Lynn; John Penny Collection, courtesy Doug Carmichael; Ransome-Wallis Collection, courtesy National Railway Museum/Science & Society Picture Library; Scottish Railway Preservation Society Archive; J. L. Stevenson Collection; Doug Carmichael; John Chamney, courtesy Norman McNab; Ewan Crawford; Mark Fielding; Late Revd Diana Forman; John Furnevel; Ian Futers; John Gray; Bill Hamilton, courtesy Mike MacDonald; Iain Henshaw; Late Patrick Howat; Alan Johnstone; Late C. Lawson Kerr, courtesy J. Stevenson; Late C. Lawson Kerr, courtesy SRPS Archive; W. Lynn; A. Mathieson; J. & C. McCutcheon Collection; Christine McGregor; Norman McNab; Tom Noble; N. E. Stead; J. Stevenson; David Stirling; Bryan Stone; P. Woods; Douglas Yuill

For my wife Christine, who has shared many West Highland journeys.

First published 2014

Amberley Publishing
The Hill, Stroud
Gloucestershire, GL5 4EP

www.amberley-books.com

ISBN 978 1 4456 3345 9 (print)
ISBN 978 1 4456 3356 5 (ebook)

British Library Cataloguing in Publication Data.
A catalogue record for this book is available from the British Library.

Typeset in 11pt on 12pt Sabon LT Std.
Typesetting by Amberley Publishing.
Printed in the UK.

CONTENTS

CHRONOLOGY

1862–3 Proposed Fort William Railway
1865 'Inverness companies' amalgamated to form Highland Railway
1865 Dingwall & Skye Railway authorised
1865 Callander & Oban Railway authorised
1870 Dingwall & Skye Railway completed to Strome Ferry (1)
1880 Callander & Oban Railway completed
1882–3 Proposed Glasgow & North Western Railway
1889 West Highland Railway Act *See below*
1890 West Highland Railway Act (supplementary) *See below*
1893 Proposed West Highland Inverlair & Kingussie Extension
1894 West Highland Railway Mallaig Extension Act
1894 West Highland opened to Fort William
1895 Banavie branch opened
1896 West Highland Railway Ballachulish Extension Act
1896 Invergarry & Fort Augustus Railway Act
1897 Loch Fyne Light Railway, Board of Trade Order
1901 Mallaig Extension opened
1903 Callander & Oban Ballachulish branch completed
1908 West Highland absorbed into North British Railway
1914 Invergarry & Fort Augustus purchased by North British Railway
1914 Invergarry & Fort Augustus Loch Ness extension abandoned
1924 North British Railway 'grouped' into London & North Eastern (2)
1933 Invergarry & Fort Augustus passenger service withdrawn
1939 Banavie branch passenger service withdrawn
1947 Invergarry & Fort Augustus closed
1948 British Railways established
1951 Banavie branch closed
1964 Arrochar & Tarbet local service withdrawn
1966 Surviving Oban services routed via Helensburgh
1984 Steam reintroduced on Mallaig extension
1988 Radio signalling introduced on West Highland lines
1989 Sprinters introduced on West Highland lines

(1) Absorbed into Highland Railway in 1880; extended to Kyle of Lochalsh in 1897.

(2) Caledonian Railway and Highland Railway 'grouped' into London, Midland & Scottish.

West Highland Railway Act, 1889 (substantive content)

Craigendoran–Crianlarich
Crianlarich–Fort William
Crianlarich, spur to Callander & Oban Railway
Fort William, foreshore

West Highland Railway Act, 1890 (substantive content)

Deviation, Glen Spean
Deviation, Torlundy–Fort William
Fort William, foreshore extension (pierhead)
Banavie branch to Caledonian Canal

On North British advice, the West Highland promoters dropped the original Caledonian Canal branch (Spean Bridge–Loch Lochy) from their 1888–9 Bill. They were denied (1889) an extension to Roshven on Loch Ailort. The West Highland Company were refused (1890) a deviation on Rannoch Moor, north of Cruach.

Map, right:
1. Crianlarich–Oban appears as a West Highland 'connection'; with the Crianlarich spur unfinished, provision of through coaches was not pursued.
2. Note 'Upper Helensburgh', 'Row', 'Inverlair'.
3. Note road connections, Bridge of Orchy–Ballachulish and Tulloch (Inverlair)–Kingussie.

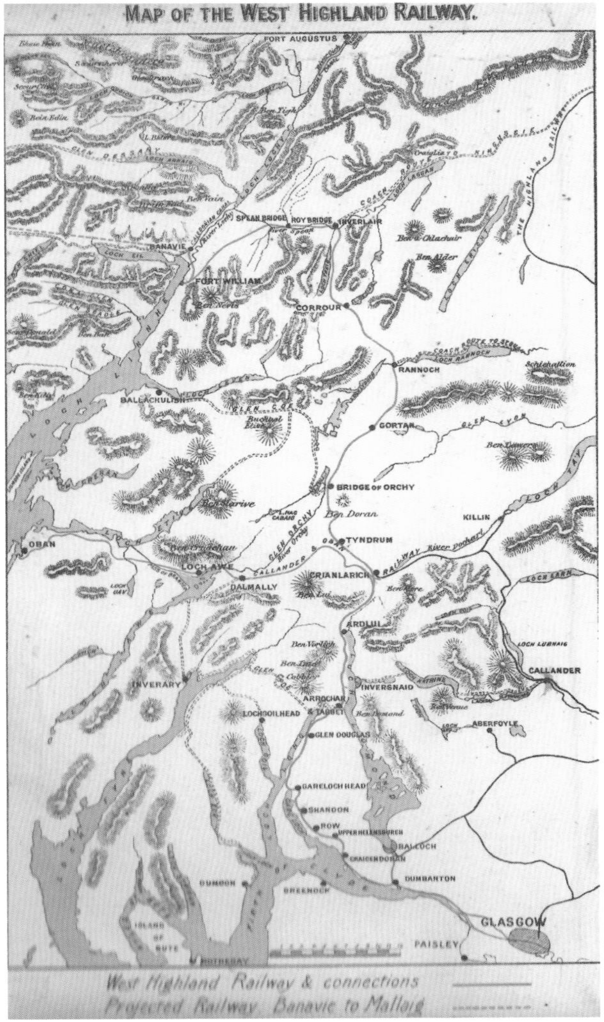

Chapter One

LOCOMOTIVES ASSOCIATED WITH THE WEST HIGHLAND RAILWAY

'West Highland Bogie' (North British Railway Class N) 231 at Fort William. Designed for the West Highland line, the class was modestly enlarged for wider use on the North British system. (Lynn)

NBR Class K (London & North Eastern Railway/British Railways Class D34) 266 *Glen Falloch* at Fort William. Curved destination boards were a North British feature. Introduced in 1913–4, the *Glens* proved generally competent but 'did their best work on the West Highland' (Hamilton-Ellis). NBR 256 *Glen Douglas*, restored in the 1950s, is now in Glasgow Transport Museum. (Alsop)

BR/LNER Class J36 (NBR Class C) 65313 at Fort William coaling stage. These 0-6-0s, dating from 1888 and subsequently rebuilt, were the first West Highland goods engines, doing occasional passenger turns, besides ballast and snow-plough work. They remained the local pilots at Fort William until the end of steam. (Stevenson)

BR/LNER Class C15 (NBR Class M) 4-4-2T 67474, 'push-pull' fitted, at Arrochar & Tarbet. The engine faces Craigendoran, ready for the return 'pull'. (Stead)

LNER Class J37 (NBR Class S) 9506 on a Down goods, between Inveruglas and Ardlui. Built from 1914 to 1921, the J37s were the North British Company's last and most powerful 0-6-0s. They undertook passenger duties when required. (Yuill)

LNER Class K2 4699 *Loch Laidon* on an Up passenger near Ardlui. The rake is all LNER 'teak'. Of the ex-Great Northern Railway 2-6-0s transferred to Scotland in the 1920s, thirteen became *Lochs.* (Stevenson)

BR/ex-LNER Class K4 61995 *Cameron of Lochiel* on a Down Extension passenger at Mallaig Junction. K4 61994 *The Great Marquess* is preserved in working condition. (Yuill)

BR Class K1 62052 at Fort William. These robust 2-6-0s, derived from the powerful but temperamental K4s, saw steam out on the West Highland route. 62005 is preserved in working condition. (Yuill)

BR/ex-LMS Class 5 ('Black 5') 44975, on a Down goods at Craigendoran, ready for the work ahead. 4-6-0s were latecomers to the West Highland and 'Black 5s', though numerous, did not overwhelm the established 2-6-0s. (Stevenson)

BR Class 27 (Type 2 BRCW built) 5359 on an Up Passenger at Ardlui in 1971. These reliable, throaty sounding Sulzers (subsequently Class 27) came to be regarded with some affection. (Furnevel)

BR Class 37 184 (English Electric Type 3) by Loch Tulla, north of Bridge of Orchy, with a 1980s summer service – a Mark 1 blue-and-grey rake with buffet car. (Stead)

Above and below: West Highland locomotives for the twenty-first century: a Class 66 shunts the oil sidings at Fort William, while a Class 67 takes the Down Sleeper over Rannoch Moor. (Fielding)

Chapter Two

GLASGOW & NORTH WESTERN

The Highland Railway Company's Tay-and-Spey main line to Inverness became, from the mid-1860s, the great artery of the North. Two cross-country lines came to link the western Highlands with the Stirling–Perth–Inverness route – the Dingwall & Skye (1870), subsequently added to the Highland Railway's system, and the Callander & Oban (1880), protégé of the powerful Caledonian Railway. The proposed Fort William Railway, an early attempt (1862–3) to connect Lochaber with the Highland main line (originally the Inverness & Perth Junction Railway) at Newtonmore, was unsuccessful.

A more direct but westerly rail route from the Central Belt to Inverness had been at least a possibility. But it ceased to be seriously considered – until in 1882–3 the Glasgow & North Western Railway was promoted. This ambitious line, 160 miles in length and estimated to cost £2 million would have run by the eastern shore of Loch Lomond, Blackmount and Glen Coe to Fort William, continuing through the Great Glen. The plans included a viaduct straddling the Glas Falls[1] in Glen Falloch; avalanche shelters beneath Glen Coe's Aonach Eagach ridge; and an uncompromising terrace along Loch Ness. It would have crossed Loch Leven not at Ballachulish Ferry but at the Dog Narrows, to double back on the northern shore. Intersecting the Callander & Oban at Crianlarich, with a connecting spur across Strathfillan to Tyndrum, it offered in addition a cut-off route to Oban, besides the later option of a branch from Fort William to the west coast.

The Glasgow & North Western was blatantly speculative, exploiting the rivalry of the Caledonian Railway and the North British and challenging the Highland's monopoly at Inverness. Though defeated, it left a legacy of suspicion, manoeuvre and pre-emptive preparations among the Scottish companies, and there was a wider context of increasing public concern over distress and unrest in the western Highlands and Islands, with transport improvement a possible remedy. From these ingredients there emerged in 1888–9 the North British-backed West Highland Railway.

1. Dramatic after rain and readily seen from West Highland trains leaving Ardlui.

Looking up Glen Falloch: the proposed line passed behind Cnap Mor (like today's West Highland Way long-distance footpath) and straddled the Glas Falls. The G&NW would have climbed from Inversaid, on the eastern shore of Loch Lomond, to its ultimate summit on Blackmount, thereafter descending by Kingshouse and Glen Coe. (Johnstone)

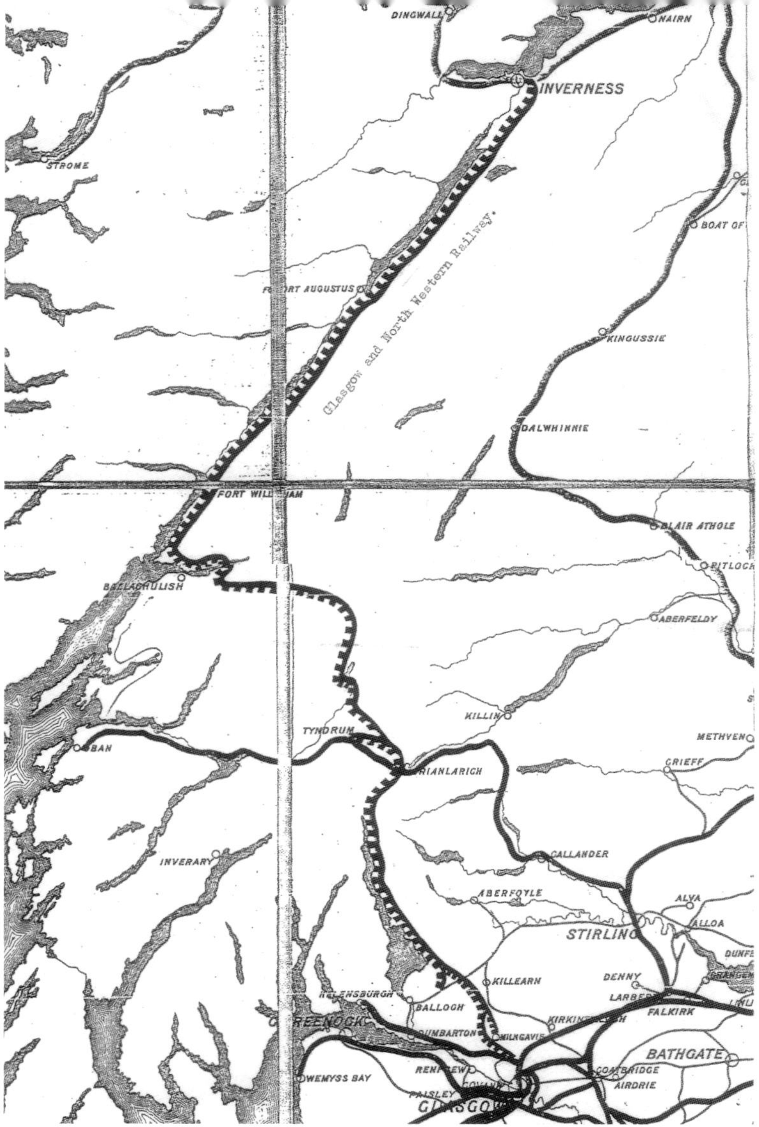

Right: Map to accompany the G&NW parliamentary plans of engineer Thomas Walrond-Smith.

Glen Coe: Walrond-Smith intended a series of short tunnels and avalanche shelters below the Aonach Eagach ridge. (Johnstone)

Dog Narrows, Loch Leven, beneath the Mamores – where the G&NW would have completed its descent, doubling back on the northern shore. (Johnstone)

Chapter Three

THE WEST HIGHLAND RAILWAY – SUCCESS

Lochaber had been repeatedly disappointed of rail connection. The Highland Company showed no enthusiasm for a Fort William branch, whether by Loch Laggan from Speyside or by the Great Glen. During the long-drawn-out construction of the Callander & Oban, hopes faded of a branch from Connel Ferry through Appin and Ballachulish. The excitement of the Glasgow & North Western scheme – in which Fort William was to become the principal intermediate station on a through line to Inverness – proved short-lived.

At the turn of 1887–8 a new campaign began. Letters to the Scottish press listed Fort William's existing means of transport, all unsatisfactory:

> By steamer via Mull of Kintyre twice a week, occupying about twenty-eight hours; by steamer via Crinan Canal and Oban, daily during the tourist season, occupying fourteen hours; by rail to Balloch, steamer on Loch Lomond, coach to Ballachulish and steamer to Fort William, during the tourist season, fourteen hours; by rail to Kingussie, and thence by coach to Fort William, daily, about fourteen hours; and by rail via Stirling and Callander to Oban, and steamer to Fort William, about eleven hours.

The Lochaber landowners at first preferred a renewed appeal to the Caledonian Railway for connection with Connel Ferry; but the hoteliers, merchants and professional men of Fort William feared permanent subordination to Oban, which, once rail-served, had grown rapidly as a market town and tourist centre. For an independent line from the Central Belt, they looked hopefully to the North British Railway. Banker and solicitor Nigel MacKenzie brought town and country together; he was well placed to do so, as agent or factor for several large estates in the western Highlands. Lord Abinger (Inverlochy) and Cameron of Lochiel set out to secure the goodwill or at least neutrality of all the proprietors along the proposed route – by the Gare Loch, Loch Long, Loch Lomond, Blackmount and Glen Coe, continuing beyond Fort William to a new harbour on the Arisaig coast. It was surveyed by Formans & McCall, already engaged by the Colquhouns of Luss to lay out a local line from Helensburgh to Garelochhead.

In Charles Forman's report (20 August 1888)[1] is the genesis of the West Highland Railway. Along the Gare Loch the line should be substantially built, as an extension of the Helensburgh Railway; beyond Garelochhead, it should be formed as cheaply as possible, with 'steep gradients and quick curves', on the model of Forman's Clyde, Ardrishaig & Crinan Railway (approved in 1887 but wound up in 1892). Locomotives 'of moderate speed' would suffice – bogie 4-4-0s with a 16-ton coupled-axle load, taking up to 150 tons at 25 mph. The landowners ought to acknowledge 'the enhancement of their properties' by giving land at nominal value and deferring claims for any interest due.

To Garelochhead	9 miles	£54,000 for works
To Crianlarich	24 miles	£96,000 for works
To Fort William (via Glen Coe)	55 miles	£220,000 for works
To West Coast (Roshven)	27 miles	£108,000 for works
Totals	115 miles	£478,000 for works
Estimate		£38,340 for land
Grand Total		£516,340

Add 15 per cent for contingencies and round up to £600,000

The sum of £600,000 was to prove a much too optimistic figure, but Forman's aim, as with his Crinan line, was almost a light railway. The North British would insist on heavier track. Moreover, in the decade after the West Highland opened, more check rails and more sleepers per rail length were put in, with the worst curves eased and reverse curves modified.

While the West Highland Bill of 1888–9 was prepared, the North British Company kept in the background but consented to a guarantee and a working and maintenance agreement. Unaware how far the scheme had matured, the Caledonian were wrong-footed, while the Highland Company chose to negotiate (see Chapter Ten). Modified to cross Rannoch Moor, entering Lochaber from the north-east, Forman's Craigendoran–Fort William line was authorised in August 1889.

Alterations between Craigendoran and Crianlarich were agreed without difficulty. A supplementary West Highland Act (1890) covered the alterations onwards to Fort William and added a branch to Banavie. Lucas & Aird broke ground in October 1889, at Helensburgh, Arrochar, Crianlarich, Tyndrum and Fort William. A dispute with the contractors[2], which prolonged the period of construction, was resolved when the North British brought forward the purchase of Lucas & Aird's West Highland shares (which would otherwise have taken place when the line was finished). By 1893 a continuous 'impermanent' line stretched from Craigendoran to Rannoch, and the Fort William construction team, supplied entirely by sea, had built along Glen Spean and up Loch Treig side to Corrour. A last-spike ceremony was held that September at Cruach.

1. Long-hand copy of Fort William merchant Donald Boyd.

2. Between Craigendoran and Crianlarich there was more 'mixed excavation' than anticipated. Soil and rock were awkwardly mingled, when it was quicker – and cheaper – to deal with one or the other.

Before the West Highland came: harvest near Helensburgh. (McCutcheon)

Before the West Highland came: Crianlarich and the Callander & Oban station, looking east to Ben More.

Before the West Highland came: the fort, Fort William, in private hands from the 1850s, when military use ceased.

Charles Forman, engineer of the West Highland Railway. (Late Revd Diana Forman)

Chapter Four

JOURNEY, PRELUDE, GLASGOW–CRAIGENDORAN

In 1865 the North British Railway absorbed the Edinburgh & Glasgow, which had come to control the north bank of the lower Clyde. Along with railheads at Balloch (Loch Lomond) and Helensburgh, the North British inherited the 'right', haphazardly asserted by the Edinburgh & Glasgow Company, to expand at some future time into the western Highlands. Relevant here was the route chosen by the promoters of the Callander & Oban Railway and its protracted construction (1865–80); those who preferred the more direct route to Oban via Loch Lomond remained vocal.

From 1894 West Highland trains would take the Helensburgh line from Glasgow Queen Street, diverging at Craigendoran. Cable assistance out of Queen Street remained the rule until 1908. North British working timetables of the 1890s show that the late afternoon 'Fort William' might go up to Cowlairs together with the late afternoon 'Perth' (the latter running by Alloa and the Devon Valley line). The vanished island station at Cowlairs once gave snappy Edinburgh connections in and out of certain West Highland trains.[1] Services off the West Highland still paused there in the 1950s and, when double-headed, released their leading engine to Eastfield depot. But this scarcely reduced Queen Street's perpetual smoke and steam, because almost every departing train was banked up the tunnel incline.

Queen Street Low Level (on the Glasgow City & District Railway, a North British subsidiary) would eventually handle West Highland excursion and summer relief traffic, which ran via Anniesland and Westerton or via Yoker and Dalmuir. Rationalisation (with electrification) meant abandonment (1959) of the original line between Bowling and Dumbarton Central. All trains now pass through Dumbarton East, a relic of the Lanarkshire & Dumbartonshire Railway, whereby the Caledonian Company had penetrated North British preserves on the lower Clyde.

Today's standard West Highland service out of Queen Street is a two-unit four-car Sprinter, dividing at Crianlarich, whence the leading unit continues to Oban and the rear to Fort William and Mallaig. Turning west at Cowlairs, the train pauses at Dalmuir, on the city's outer edge, giving interchange with the electrified Strathclyde network. It calls at Dumbarton Central. Beyond Cardross, the Clyde estuary widens. Craigendoran Junction, where the West Highland commences, is approached on a long curve.

1. The earliest West Highland timetables also show Edinburgh and Glasgow portions uniting at Dumbarton.

North British Railway Hotel, George Square, Glasgow – convenient over many years for those who took the early Glasgow Queen Street–Mallaig train, with same-day steamer connection to Skye and Lewis. (Alsop)

Two 'Black 5s' head a 1950s West Highland departure. BR's carmine-and-cream coach livery prevails. (Stevenson)

A BRCW Type 2, 27 038, brings the morning Mallaig–Glasgow, which added a van and buffet car at Fort William, through Cowlairs North Junction in May 1978.The East Junction–North Junction spur (behind the signalbox) allows Edinburgh trains to access the West Highland without reversal. (Noble)

An Up train of the 1890s (three coaches and brake van was standard) behind 'West Highland Bogie' 343, is captured near Garscadden (taking the Yoker line from Dalmuir, and not the normal route via Westerton). (Hennigan collection, courtesy Lynn)

The Up West Highland Sleeper, since 1989 an independent train, at Dalmuir. (Crawford)

Today's Craigendoran Junction – where the West Highland begins. The original line, continuing to Helensburgh Central and long electrified, is now single; the West Highland island platform has gone; at bottom right are the remains of the steamer pier. (Crawford)

Chapter Five

JOURNEY (1)

From sea-level at Craigendoran, the West Highland at once climbs steeply (1 in 58) to Helensburgh Upper, where the gradient eases. Topping the minor summit near Rhu, the line follows the hillside above the Gare Loch, rounding Faslane bay into Garelochhead and climbing once more (1 in 60). A pronounced geological fault runs obliquely from the Clyde estuary to the east coast, and Garelochhead is something of a frontier between Lowlands and Highlands. Ahead the landscape becomes mountainous, and the gradient is continuous (stiffening in part to 1 in 54) all the way to Glen Douglas summit (564 feet).

Cutting the base of the Roseneath peninsula, the line emerges on Lochlongside, above Portincaple and opposite Loch Goil. Past Finnart, it turns inland by Glen Mallan. Through Glen Douglas passing place and once more above Loch Long, on a falling gradient (1 in 57) to Arrochar & Tarbet, it finds a vertiginous but tree-clad terrace. The rock face, much patched and buttressed, looms over the trains. Across the water, Ben Arthur (The Cobbler) appears behind Glen Croe, towering over the road to Loch Fyne. At Arrochar & Tarbet, Ben Lomond becomes the principal landmark. To the south, Loch Lomond opens out; northward it points a finger, which road and railway follow, past Craigroyston and Inversnaid on the opposite shore. Through Inveruglas and beneath Ben Vorlich,[1] these relatively easy miles include, at Craigenarden, the West Highland's only arched viaduct and (as first built) only tunnel; the line is more-or-less level, finally dipping into Ardlui.

Now comes the unrelenting 7-mile ascent of Glen Falloch (largely at 1 in 65). Inverarnan lies in the valley bottom, an important 'stance' when droving flourished, and once accessible from the Clyde via the Vale of Leven and Loch Lomond, by the canalised mouth of the River Falloch. The line curves into the side-valley gouged by the Dubh Eas burn and back into the main glen, above the Falls of Falloch. Beyond Derrydarroch, it hugs the diminishing river, which at last bends away into the mountains. Crossing the watershed of Clyde and Tay, it drops to Crianlarich, where Fillan Water, becoming the River Dochart, leads eastward to Killin and Loch Tay. Over seven decades of steam traction, the approach to Crianlarich was the 'fireman's rest', a brief respite from the shovel. Strathfillan is an ancient crossroads: the modern highways, south–north and east–west, combine at Crianlarich and part company again at Tyndrum.

1. The other Ben Vorlich, near Strathyre, was a Callander & Oban landmark.

Chapter Six

JOURNEY (2)

The West Highland, leaving Crianlarich, strides across Strathfillan to resume (at 1 in 60) the long climb begun at Ardlui, while the now truncated Callander & Oban has the easier alignment on the opposite slopes. In the rear, Ben More and Stobinian dominate Glen Dochart. Past Auchtertyre, Ben Lui appears to the west, and the line comes abruptly to Upper Tyndrum[1] – an appropriate designation, the access road being dauntingly steep. Evidence remains of lead mining in former times. Recent decades have seen the village become a service point for road transport, especially tourist coaches, to rival Crianlarich. On the West Highland comes the final stint to County March summit (1,024 feet), while the Callander & Oban turns away westward into Glen Lochy.

As earlier at Glen Douglas, ascent alters unmistakably to descent. With Ben Dorain ahead, the line drops (at 1 in 55) towards Auch, revealing the celebrated 'Horseshoe', which curves from mountainside to mountainside – in, round and out again for Bridge of Orchy, while the gradient eases (to 1 in 150). The West Highland has crossed another watershed. Draining Loch Tulla, and fed both from Blackmount and from Rannoch, the River Orchy flows west to Loch Awe and saltwater Loch Etive. At Achallader the modern road turns away for Glen Coe and Fort William; but the railway tends north-east, from Glen Orchy, by Tulla Water, into Rannoch Moor.

The ascent of Strathtulla (1 in 60) levels off beyond Crannach Wood. Beyond Gorton[2] passing place – where the loop, removed but then restored, is nowadays reserved for engineering use – the line undulates across the moorland and through a maturing plantation into the shallow valley of the River Gauer, which deepens eastward towards invisible Loch Rannoch. Somewhere, among peat hags and sluggish streams, the West Highland has re-entered the vast Tay catchment. From Rannoch station the narrow road, built in conjunction with the railway, runs east to Kinlochrannoch and Pitlochry.

1. Altered from BR's 'Tyndrum Upper', for radio-signalling security. 'Tyndrum Lower' (Oban line) is retained.

2. Originally Gortan.

Chapter Seven

JOURNEY (3)

By a short, stiff climb (1 in 53) round the flanks of Cruach Hill, with Schiehallion briefly in view, the line emerges from Cruach snow-shed, on to the northern reaches of the moor and past the outliers of Ben Alder. The prospect westward widens, from the Black Corries behind little Loch Chlaidheimh to the distant mountains of Glen Coe. The final watershed is, once again, imperceptible. But the Blackwater flows west to Loch Leven, while Loch Ossian and Loch Treig gather the burns on either side of Corrour; both are tributary to the Laggan-Spean-Lochy system, emptying into Loch Linnhe at Fort William. Though that destination is as yet 30 miles away, the West Highland has found its roundabout way into Lochaber.

From Corrour summit (1,347 feet), just beyond Corrour station, the railway curves downhill to Lochtreighead, whence the descent is steady (for the most part at 1 in 67) to Fersit and into Glen Spean. With ugly scour marks save when brimming full, Loch Treig has been some eighty years a reservoir. A short tunnel marks the deviation which this necessitated. (In the right conditions the original trackbed can still be traced.) From Tulloch, after the reverse curves at Inverlair Falls, the line heads decisively south-west through Brae Lochaber. A main road, the first such since Achallader, once more keeps company. As the downhill gradient eases (to 1 in 126), the valley widens – then contracts into dramatic Monessie Gorge.

Roy Bridge to Spean Bridge, crossing the River Spean, is a 3-mile canter, which imparts a sense of journey's end. But to follow the Spean into the Great Glen, where it merges with the River Lochy, would be a detour; instead the course of road and railway parallels the Great Glen proper, over the minor summit at Auchendaul. A brief climb (1 in 100), a longer descent (steepening to 1 in 80), and the line rounds the Torlundy curves, below the cliffs of Ben Nevis. Fort William's 'suburbia' takes shape ahead – the town possessed scarcely 1,500 inhabitants a century ago, but the built-up area now extends through Inverlochy to Caol, Banavie and Corpach: past the aluminium smelter and past the junction where the Mallaig line trails in (see Chapter Nine), the Sprinter comes to rest in the 'new' station (in fact commissioned nearly forty years ago and since refurbished).

Upper reaches of Glen Falloch. (Johnstone)

Achallader, Strathtulla, beneath Ben an Dothaidh and Ben Achaladair – seen from Blackmount. (Johnstone)

Sprinter Journey Today

Right: On the margin of the Clydeside conurbation, the abrupt climb to Helensburgh Upper presages the gradients beyond Garelochhead. (Crawford)

Below left: Past Whistlefield the ascent to Glen Douglas stiffens as Loch Long appears below, with Loch Goil opposite. (McNab)

Below right: Out of Crianlarich and across Fillan Water, into Strathfillan. (Crawford)

Dwarfed by wintry Ben Dorain, descending from County March into the 'Horseshoe'. (Fielding)

From Corrour to Lochtreighead, thence into Glen Spean, the line quits Rannoch Moor for Brae Lochaber. (Fielding)

The River Gauer, flowing east from Loch Laidon to Loch Rannoch, relieves the miles of bog and conifer south of Rannoch station. (Gray)

Arrival into Fort William, past the signal box once designated 'Banavie Junction'. Here semaphores remain, though RETB, now some twenty-five years established, is otherwise the rule all the way from Helensburgh Upper to Mallaig. (Henshaw)

Chapter Eight

OPENING DAY AND CENTENARY

Completion for the summer of 1894 was a very near thing. Vast quantities of 'fill' were required to consolidate the line on Rannoch Moor, and the 'big banks' approaching the Gauer and Rannoch viaducts were troublesome. ('Still sinking yesterday and today going straight down, hardly fit for big engine', reported Lucas & Aird's section engineer, just a month before opening day.) The scale of the task was daunting, not the technique – which included lengths of 'floating' embankment, founded on brushwood rafts. Ballast trains (on which North British enginemen learned their new railway) could not reach Rannoch until the viaducts to the south were ready. And a July thunderstorm washed out the formation near Achallader, in the presence of Major Marindin RE, the Board of Trade inspector, who was making his penultimate, week-long examination of the line. An empty ballast train fell into the gap and its fireman was fatally injured.

Notwithstanding this embarrassment, on Friday 3 August 1894 the final inspection ended satisfactorily, subject to adjustment of points and signals during that weekend. On Monday 6th the contractor's locomotives and rolling stock were, as far as possible, withdrawn. Sets of the new bogie coaches dedicated to the West Highland, which had been stored for several months, were run back and forth to ease the axle-boxes, with two sets stabled at Fort William, ready for the public service (three daily trains in each direction) which began on 7 August. The official opening ceremony, tentatively planned for June and then July, was hastily confirmed for the following Saturday, 11 August. On Friday 10th a special train came north, carrying a dozen waiters, a marquee, tables and chairs, potted plants, and food and drink. In charge was 'Mr Rupprecht of the North British Station Hotel, Glasgow'.

The opening day special, eleven coaches hauled by two 'West Highland Bogies', was timed so as not to delay the regular trains – which it crossed at Arrochar & Tarbet and Inverlair (Tulloch) on the Down journey, and at Inverlair (again) and Ardlui on the Up. Aboard were 350 guests, including North British directors and departmental heads, with their wives; emissaries of the other Scottish railway companies; and Charles Forman and John Aird, with representatives of their engineering staffs. Fort William's partially completed station was kept for the public service, and a temporary platform awaited the special, opposite the old fort, where a gated heather arch had been thrown over the main line, sturdy enough to carry bagpipers on its mock battlements. Operating convenience apart, it was politic to avoid the pierhead terminus. Though a truce prevailed for the long-awaited opening, the burgh would continue to contest the West Highland's occupation of the foreshore (see Chapter Fourteen).

The Marquess of Tweeddale, who chaired both the North British Company and the West Highland, presided. Hopes of a royal occasion had generated an anxious correspondence. Could Cameron of Lochiel 'put up' the Duke of York (the future George V) at Achnacarry? Would Princess Louise, wife of the Marquess of Lorne, be more amenable? In the end the official ceremony was performed by the Marchioness of Tweeddale – not royal but appropriately experienced – who in 1890 had 'driven' (the real driver at her elbow) the first train across the newly opened Forth Bridge. With a silver key she unlocked the ornamental gates, which were swung clear of the line. Amid exploding fog signals and the skirl of pipes, the special steamed slowly through the arch.

In the marquee some 400 people, local dignitaries included, sat down to lunch, which culminated in a round of toasts and speeches – formidable in that little more than three hours were allowed for both ceremony and banquet. (The special, which had arrived half an hour late, departed only a little behind time.) Tea was served during the seven-minute pause scheduled at Rannoch. Just how this was contrived is something of a mystery.

In 1994, centenary celebrations were put in doubt by industrial action (a signalmen's dispute). It was once again a near thing. The author's *100 Years of the West Highland Railway* was hastily commissioned by ScotRail amid the hectic preparations for privatisation (cf. how in 1944 wartime regulations had constrained George Dow's *The Story of the West Highland* – the LNER's fiftieth anniversary production). But the commemorative special of 1994 ran as planned, behind two EE Class 37s. At Fort William guests and townsfolk looked on as restored ex-LNER K4 *The Great Marquess* passed beneath a replica arch. A latter-day banquet took place in An Aird Centre, one of the new public buildings in the area reclaimed and developed north of today's station, following diversion of the River Nevis. An Aird until the 1970s was a tidal wasteland, the backdrop to what are now period photographs of the vanished railway yard and engine shed at the old fort.

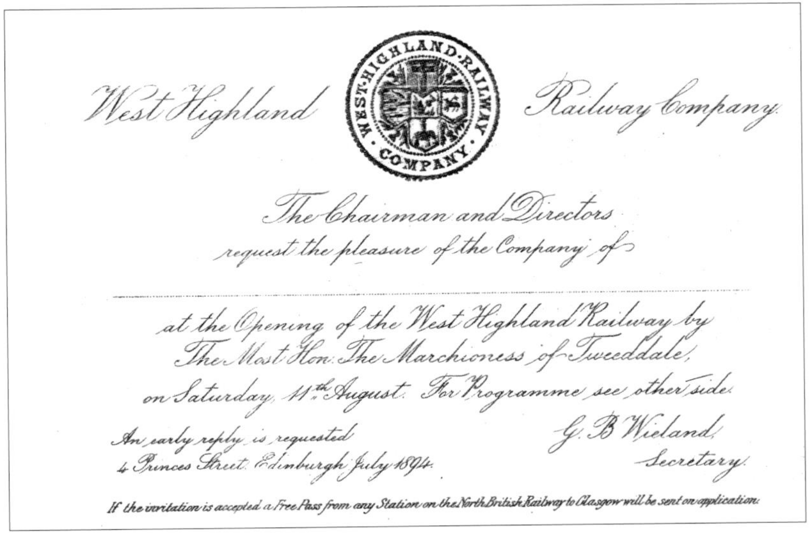

West Highland Railway Company

WEST HIGHLAND RAILWAY COMPANY

The Chairman and Directors
request the pleasure of the Company of

....

at the Opening of the West Highland Railway by
The Most Hon: The Marchioness of Tweeddale,
on Saturday, 11th August. For Programme see other side.

An early reply is requested
4 Princes Street, Edinburgh July 1894.

G. B. Wieland
Secretary.

If the invitation is accepted a Free Pass from any Station on the North British Railway to Glasgow will be sent on application.

Opening day invitation.

Railwaymen beside 'West Highland Bogie' 701: the opening day special waits empty at Fort William's temporary platform. (Gillespie)

Centenary Special at Spean Bridge, 11 August 1994. (Christine McGregor)

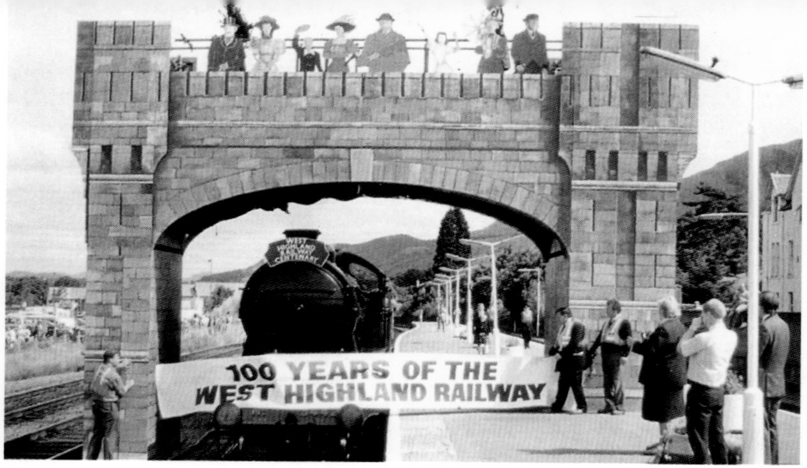

Opening day re-enacted, 11 August 1994, by *The Great Marquess*, in LNER green. (Stevenson)

Commemorative postcard, 1994: 'West Highland Bogie' 695 with West Highland Company seal and North British Company badge.

Chapter Nine

THE WEST HIGHLAND MALLAIG EXTENSION

The West Highland Company set a UK record by opening all at once 100 miles of railway, touching no community of any size along the way and without any connections north of Craigendoran (save the Banavie branch and the Crianlarich spur, both as yet unfinished). The North British made some play with this unprecedented achievement – general manager John Conacher having checked his facts with Bradshaw – as emphasising their commitment to a neglected region where a paying traffic would take time to develop. It was a heavy hint that government should recognise the sacrifice involved.

In 1888–9 the West Highland Bill had included an extension from Fort William to a new harbour at Roshven on saltwater Loch Ailort. This met the prescription of the Napier Commission (1882–3) that a third railhead for the Hebrides, additional to Oban and Strome (the then terminus of the Dingwall & Skye), was desirable: if private enterprise were to bring a railway to Lochaber, it ought to be extended westward with state aid. The North British guarantee did not embrace the Roshven line, which was expendable (though at some risk to the whole West Highland project), a marker for the future when a considered government policy for the Highlands and Islands had emerged. Transport subsidies, for mail steamers and for additional railways, were recommended by the Lothian Commission (1889–90) and by the subsequent Treasury Committee (1890–1).

The Roshven project had been revived (1891) in more ambitious form as the 'Loch Eil & Mallaig Railway', soon to be known as the West Highland Mallaig Extension; and from 1893 the North British were prepared to endorse it, conditional on state assistance. The Mallaig line was authorised in August 1894, with the West Highland just about to open; but the vital Treasury guarantee hung fire into 1896. Construction of the 41-mile extension, subsuming the first mile of the Banavie branch (see Chapter Ten), began early in 1897. Arched viaducts in mass concrete contrasted with the girder spans on slender masonry piers which characterised the older line; eleven tunnels were required between Kinlocheil and Arisaig, against the solitary example on Lochlomondside. Station buildings were simpler but kept a family resemblance to the earlier West Highland 'chalets'.

Opening came in April 1901. The basic West Highland timetable would be defined for the next seventy years by Mallaig's steamer connections with Skye and Lewis, while Mallaig fish added usefully to West Highland revenue. Travel between Glasgow and Fort William offers much variety, but the shorter journey onwards to the coast was recognised from the first as a scenic experience without equal: on this the fame of the Mallaig line still rests, powerfully reinforced by the revival since 1984 of 'heritage steam'. Though this book is a celebration of the West Highland proper, the extension must occasionally feature in the pages which follow.

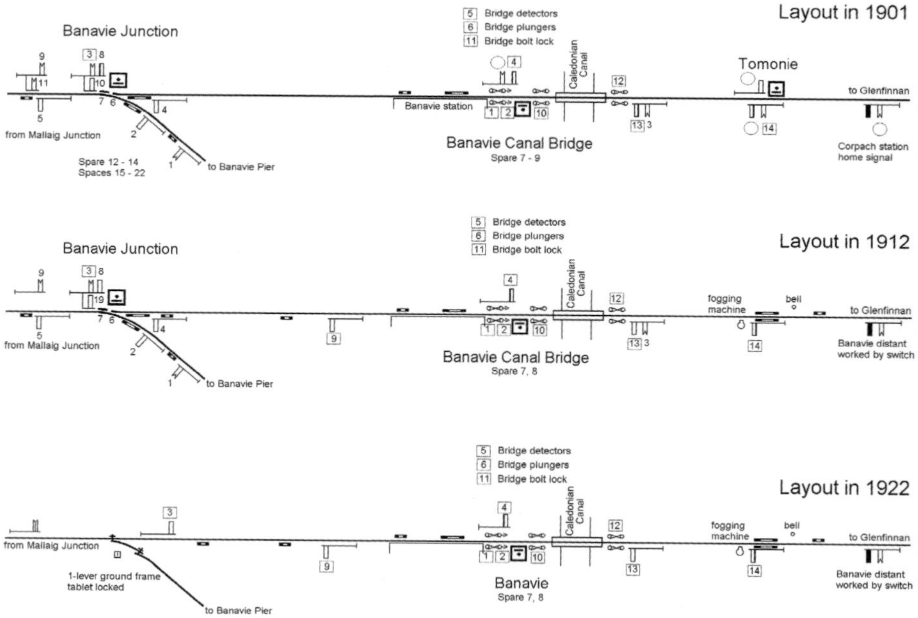

Above: A fish 'empties' for Mallaig, in charge of BR/ex-LNER K2 61782 *Loch Eil*, pauses at Glenfinnan. (Stevenson)

Right: Signalling diagram, Banavie Branch and Mallaig line: second 'Banavie Junction', 'Banavie Canal Bridge' and 'Tomonie' signalboxes (the last soon eliminated). With tablet-locking, the truncated branch could be worked by 'one engine in steam'. (Stirling)

The Down *Jacobite* (see Chapter 29) on Loch Eilt causeway. (Fielding)

Fish vans on Mallaig's breakwater-cum-pier in 1958, with MacBrayne vessels *Loch Mor* and *Loch Nevis*. (Chamney, courtesy McNab)

Chapter Ten

BANAVIE BRANCH

The West Highland project, as presented to Parliament in 1888–9, did not invade the Highland Company's heartland; and with Roshven struck out by the House of Lords[1] there was no immediate threat to the Highland's Hebridean traffic via Strome Ferry. Caledonian and Highland had stood together against the Glasgow & North Western scheme, but this time the latter chose compromise and did not renew their opposition when the West Highland Bill reached the Commons. The Great Glen Agreement (or Ten Years' Truce) was brokered by the North British and forbad a West Highland advance to Inverness for a full decade after traffic to Fort William began. Highland fears were allayed, too, when the West Highland promoters dropped their proposed branch from Spean Bridge to Loch Lochy, on the Caledonian Canal – it was suspect as a tentative thrust towards Inverness. Under the agreement, the Highland accepted a West Highland branch to Banavie, for rail and steamer interchange at the southern end of the canal, judging this to be harmless.

The 1½-mile Banavie branch made a trailing junction with the Torlundy–Fort William deviation – both were authorised by the West Highland Act of 1890. The branch crossed the River Lochy by a handsome viaduct, clearly of a kind with the masonry-and-girder structures which characterise the West Highland proper north from Garelochhead, but distinctive in that the spans are partially sunk into the castellated piers. Embellishment on the West Highland was sparing, in this instance intended to 'match' the nearby ruins of Inverlochy Castle, dating from the fourteenth century. (As approved in 1889, the West Highland would have entered Fort William along the Lochy; the Roshven line, had it been included, would have bridged the estuary at the islands downstream from the present viaduct.)

From 1901, the line thus far was to become the stem of the West Highland Mallaig Extension. The final half-mile remained a branch, curving to the canal on a rising embankment. By an abrupt ascent and back shunt, a luggage van could be brought alongside the pier at Banavie upper basin, which stood above the station. Passengers took the short footpath. Here, eastbound craft completed the ascent of the dramatic Neptune's Staircase and those westbound began their descent. The eight conjoined locks achieved a 64-foot rise or fall, but negotiating them was tedious. While cargo steamers worked from Liverpool or Glasgow through to Inverness, David MacBrayne's passenger vessels turned in the upper basin. In summer a 'horse omnibus' had connected with Corpach, where the Oban mail steamers terminated. Now, tourists could disembark at Fort William and transfer by train, perhaps breaking their journey overnight.

Ostensibly a substitute for the Loch Lochy link deleted in 1889, the branch also made a statement – that the Roshven line, or some equivalent, would be revived as soon as possible, continuing from Banavie through Corpach and Glenfinnan to the coast. In the meantime Banavie became a railhead for the districts to the west. Certain Glasgow trains began or terminated there, reversing in Fort William. A siding and crane were provided for goods traffic – which included distillers' grain from the Black Isle and Moray, shipped down the canal and 'tripped' by rail. Though the main road led directly to Ben Nevis distillery, little over a mile away, weight restrictions on the then suspension bridge over the Lochy made carting costly and rail worthwhile.

The working timetable for July 1896 shows a goods to Banavie at 5.40 a.m., returning as a mixed train to connect with the 6.20 a.m. for Glasgow. There were eight passenger workings out and back throughout the day, taking nine minutes in each direction, the last at 10 p.m. in connection with the late afternoon Down service from Edinburgh and Glasgow. With a new 'Banavie' on the extension, adjacent to the lower basin, the original station became 'Banavie Pier'. (Thereafter the branch timetable shrank to a very basic provision; ultimately, the summer 'boat train' ran just three days a week.) The original 'Banavie Junction' signal box became 'Mallaig Junction'.[2] For Extension traffic, a new 'Banavie Junction' was paired with 'Tomonie', over the canal, while 'Banavie Canal Bridge', in between, controlled only the bridge. At first inflexible, the Board of Trade subsequently recognised that such elaborate protection was unnecessary, and Banavie Canal Bridge became the tablet box, eliminating Tomonie.

Elderly rigid-wheelbase rolling stock, both four-wheel and six-wheel, was considered adequate for the Banavie branch in its early years (and for the first local trains on the Mallaig Extension). Passenger trains to Banavie Pier ceased from 1939 and the branch closed entirely in 1951. The low-lying land between the River Lochy and the canal, known as Corpach Moss (or the Blar Mhor) and occupied by a few crofts, has been gradually built up and road alterations have largely obliterated the branch earth works. The station building, for years dilapidated, has been transformed into a modern dwelling.

1. Having opposed the West Highland Bill in the House of Lords, the Highland did not renew their opposition in the Commons.

2. Renamed a second time, it is now 'Fort William Junction'. The original Fort William box vanished in the upheaval of the 1970s (see Chapter Fourteen).

2005 on Lochy viaduct, looking to Inverlochy Castle and Ben Nevis. (Gray)

Banavie, branch terminus, 1895 – from 1901, Banavie Pier. (Stevenson)

NBR Class R 4-4-0T 1405 and luggage van, run in connection with the Caledonian Canal steamers: this required a back shunt to Banavie basin. (Stevenson)

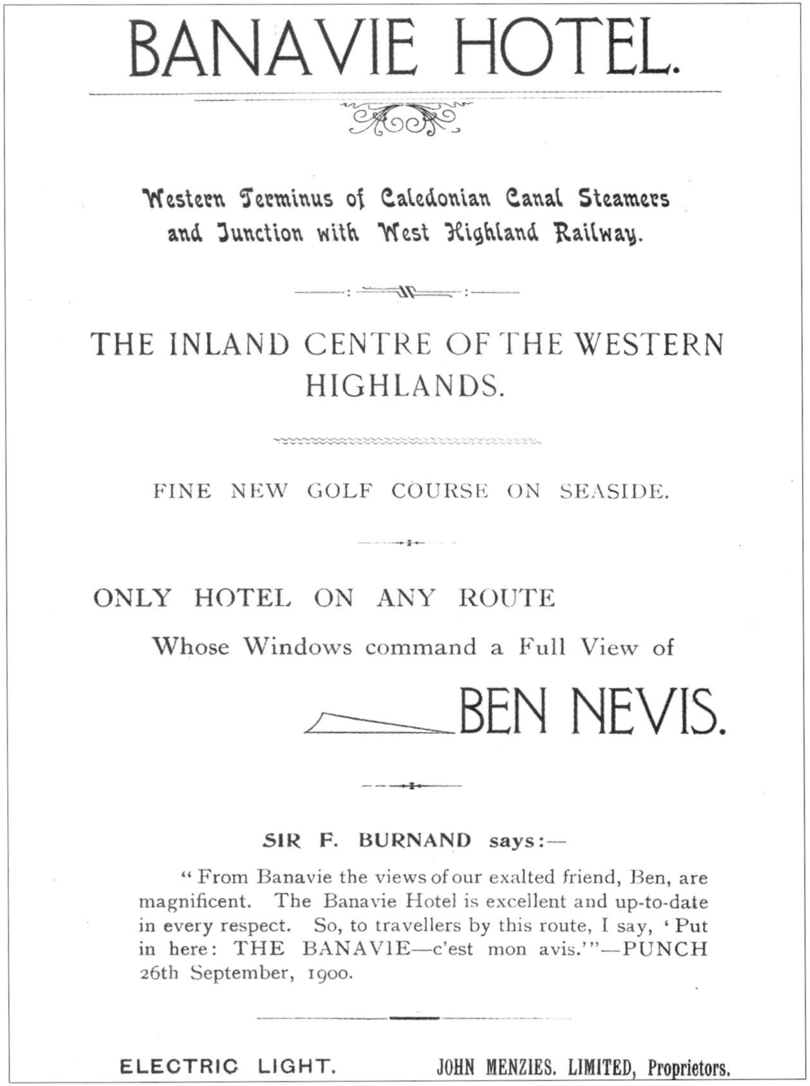

BANAVIE HOTEL.
Western Terminus of Caledonian Canal Steamers
and Junction with West Highland Railway.
THE INLAND CENTRE OF THE WESTERN HIGHLANDS.
FINE NEW GOLF COURSE ON SEASIDE.
ONLY HOTEL ON ANY ROUTE
Whose Windows command a Full View of
BEN NEVIS.
SIR F. BURNAND says:—
" From Banavie the views of our exalted friend, Ben, are magnificent. The Banavie Hotel is excellent and up-to-date in every respect. So, to travellers by this route, I say, ' Put in here: THE BANAVIE—c'est mon avis.' "—PUNCH 26th September, 1900.
ELECTRIC LIGHT.
JOHN MENZIES, LIMITED, Proprietors.

Advertisement for Banavie Hotel (the sometime 'Lochiel Arms'), 1907. (SRPS)

Chapter Eleven

THE INVERGARRY & FORT AUGUSTUS RAILWAY

At the West Highland's opening day (see Chapter Eight), Lord Tweeddale declared that the Mallaig Extension was now the North British Company's prime concern. He urged the reluctant Liberal Government to legislate for the state assistance which their Conservative predecessors had pledged in 1892.[1] He implied that the Great Glen Agreement with the Highland Railway Company would remain in being. By its terms, there could be no Fort William–Inverness line before 1904.

That the agreement had been challenged only months earlier went unmentioned. In the autumn of 1893, amid rumours of a speculative promotion echoing the Glasgow & North Western, engineer Charles Forman had surveyed a line through the Great Glen and canvassed prospective backers. He also surveyed a link along Loch Laggan, from the West Highland in Glen Spean to the Highland main line in Strathspey. The Highland Railway and the North British were divided by the Mallaig Extension Bill;[2] but, contrary to Forman's expectations, their Ten Years' Truce survived. The two general managers (Andrew Dougall and John Conacher), at odds over Mallaig in their public statements and parliamentary evidence, nevertheless concurred behind the scenes – a no-man's land should be preserved between Inverness and Fort William. To this end the North British would endorse, and the Highland tolerate, Forman's Spean-and-Spey scheme – an option which the Great Glen Agreement left open. In the event, the Laggan line had not been lodged, though the *Edinburgh Gazette* gave notice of an impending 'West Highland Inverlair & Kingussie Extension Bill'. No Great Glen promotion materialised.

These alarms receded during the final push to make the West Highland ready for traffic, but a crisis came within weeks of Tweeddale's speech. The rumours of the previous year redoubled, and the Highland Railway, fearing North British treachery and the sudden unveiling of a new assault on Inverness, chose pre-emptive action. Denouncing the Truce, the Highland now brought forward a Fort William Extension Bill, so as to block the Great Glen with a line surveyed by their own engineer. The North British replied with a West Highland Inverness Extension Bill (for which Forman's plans were hastily purchased – there ws no scheme ready, and the Highland had been over-nervous). Negotiations restored the 1889 agreement early in 1895. With the competing schemes both withdrawn, the Great Glen was once more 'locked up', to the resentment of local people. The about-turn lost the West Highland much goodwill. Less had been expected of the Highland Company, who sought only to bar the way to Inverness and would have postponed construction.

The promoters of the Invergarry & Fort Augustus Railway, which won parliamentary approval in 1896 despite the strenuous opposition of the Highland Railway and the North British, had set out to destroy the agreement once and for all. The Spean Bridge–Fort Augustus line was ostensibly a landowners' project, compatible with any larger scheme which might eventually be pursued; in the meantime, as a feeder to the West Highland, it would benefit the proprietors, their 'sportsman' tenants and all the Great Glen communities lacking rail connection with the Highland system. This was disingenuous. The Invergarry & Fort Augustus needed – and obtained – speculative 'outside' capital. If the Truce were undermined a second time, Highland or North British could be constrained, in defence of their own preserves, to buy out the little company at the asking price and complete a westerly (i.e. West Highland-cum-Great Glen) line to Inverness.

During 1896–7 both Highland and North British began negotiations with the newly established Invergarry & Fort Augustus Company, while all three submitted almost identical schemes to fill the remaining 30-mile gap along Loch Ness; but the triangular contest proved inconclusive. (Parliament endorsed the Highland Company's Bill but declined to approve a railway which the Highland so manifestly did not want to build.) Confident that offers to purchase would be renewed sooner or later, the Invergarry & Fort Augustus now devoted all their resources to completing their authorised 22-mile line, which made junction with the West Highland at Spean Bridge. In fact, they had less leverage than they supposed. Though the Great Glen Agreement was indeed defunct, for the Highland Railway and the North British the 'non-result' of 1897 was not unwelcome, and an unacknowledged truce continued until 1901, when the Invergarry & Fort Augustus was ready for traffic.

After a barren and expensive struggle over operating rights, in 1903 the Highland moved in: locomotives, rolling stock and equipment were brought via Perth and Crianlarich to work and maintain the Spean Bridge–Fort Augustus line, isolated from their own system. In 1907, convinced that Inverness was no longer threatened, they would move out. The North British, by now satisfied that no twist of events could bring the Highland to Fort William, took over – which was at least a more rational solution, with some economy in running costs. Neither arrangement offered the Invergarry & Fort Augustus Company any prospect of solvency. By 1913–4, the choice was abandonment or sale to the North British at little more than scrap value. A small 'sweetener' from Inverness-shire County Council saw the purchase was concluded.

1. Very broadly speaking, the Conservatives (Unionists) were persuaded that by stimulating economic development in the Highlands and Islands they might curb agitation and avoid more radical measures, while the Liberals wanted fundamental land reform and were in principle opposed to subsidy.

2. Denied a late bill in 1892–3, following the Conservative promise of subsidy, the West Highland Company finally achieved their Mallaig Extension Act in the following parliamentary session.

NORTH BRITISH RAILWAY.

GENERAL MANAGER'S OFFICE,
EDINBURGH, *April* 1907.

CIRCULAR $\frac{G.M.}{}$

Invergarry and Fort Augustus Railway.

The Staff are hereby informed that this Company will take over the working of the above Railway on WEDNESDAY, 1ST PROXIMO.

The names of the Stations on the Line are as follows, viz. :—

Gairlochy,
Invergarry,
Aberchalder,
Fort Augustus.

Goods and Passenger Traffic can be dealt with at each of the Stations named, with the exception of Aberchalder, which is a purely "Passenger" Station; no Goods, Parcels, or Miscellaneous Traffic being dealt with.

W. F. JACKSON,
General Manager.

Acknowledgment to be signed, cut off, and returned to General Manager's Office, Edinburgh, by first available Train.

I hereby acknowledge to have received one copy of Circular $\frac{G.M.}{}$ dated April 1907, in reference to "Invergarry and Fort Augustus Railway," to which I shall attend.

*Signature,*________________

*Designation,*________________

*Station,*________________

*Date,*________________1907.

TO THE GENERAL MANAGER,
EDINBURGH.

(-C)

LNER Class C15 (ex-North British Class M) 9155 4-4-2T on a one-coach train at Fort Augustus in the last years of passenger service. A redundant signal marks the short-lived 'extension' to the I&FA's Loch Ness pier. (Casserley)

Having worked the I&FAR from 1903, the Highland Company moved out in 1907 – when the North British moved in.

Road improvement in the Great Glen, with the weak bridges over the Caledonian Canal replaced, encouraged bus operators and doomed the never profitable Fort Augustus line. (Robert Grieves Collection, courtesy Sinclair)

Remains of Oich Viaduct, Fort Augustus. The short but expensive Loch Ness 'extension' crossed both the Caledonian Canal and the River Oich. (Gray)

Chapter Twelve

WEST HIGHLAND BALLACHULISH EXTENSION

Carefully avoiding commitment, Lord Tweeddale in his opening day speech of August 1894 suggested that something would be done eventually for the districts south of Fort William, disappointed of a 'direct' line through Glen Coe when the West Highland was taken across Rannoch. But the Callander & Oban Company at once set the pace, commissioning Charles Forman[1] to survey a line from Connel Ferry through Benderloch and Appin to Ballachulish, Fort William and Banavie. The Highland Company's Bill for an Inverness–Fort William line, lodged that November (see Chapter Ten), was to include a Banavie spur. Thus the message was clear: in backing the West Highland, the North British had threatened the interests of the Highland Railway and the Callander & Oban; now they might join hands in Lochaber to challenge the North British.

Likewise ominous (for the North British) was the Caledonian Company's argument (citing practice on the state-aided lines of Ireland) that a Treasury guarantee would make the as yet unbuilt Mallaig line a 'government road' which no one company should monopolise. Joint operation of the Mallaig Extension west from Banavie had no place in North British thinking. Their anxiety subsided, however, when the Great Glen Agreement was refashioned (see Chapter Eleven). Meanwhile, the Ballachulish–Banavie scheme was put on hold. In 1891, after twenty years of intermittent warfare, Caledonian and North British had at last achieved a grudging but meaningful détente with their New Lines Agreement, which prescribed judicial arbitration in all territorial disputes. It would be twice renewed on to 1914. The arbiter had already found that Fort William and Mallaig 'belonged' to the North British and he now ruled (January 1895) that the Caledonian should restrain the Callander & Oban.

Not without bickering, a boundary was drawn at Loch Leven. The Callander & Oban might advance to Ballachulish Ferry, the West Highland to North Ballachulish: both might tap the Ballachulish slate quarries, by a joint tramway, and share the tourist business of Glen Coe. The proposed swing bridge carrying the tramway across the Ballachulish Narrows was touted as a useful road link, and through rail traffic was not envisaged – these were two branch lines meeting at a common frontier but feeding their respective parent routes, both roundabout and ultimately vulnerable to twentieth-century road competition. The prospective Oban–Fort William–Inverness rail link briefly glimpsed in 1894–5 (above) now vanished for all time.

The Callander & Oban branch to Ballachulish Ferry and the West Highland Ballachulish Extension (*sic*) both achieved parliamentary approval in 1896, but the swing bridge that would have united them (after a fashion) was disallowed, making a common tramway impossible. In 1897 the Callander & Oban obtained powers to take their line on to Ballachulish village and the adjacent quarries; it opened in 1903. The West Highland branch would never be built, though the North British twice sought the renewal of the West Highland's powers to build. This was insurance. It had become sufficient that neither the Highland Railway nor the Caledonian (Callander & Oban) should penetrate to Fort William – which in turn ensured that the West Highland Mallaig Extension would remain exclusively North British.

The line to North Ballachulish would have served Onich, which was becoming a 'residential' outpost for Fort William – the steamer service in summer was generous enough to allow commuting. A station at Corran Ferry was offered as a railhead for Ardgour, Kingairloch and Morvern. Travel to Glasgow via Fort William would have been extremely circuitous, but goods and livestock business was in prospect, besides passengers. The Caledonian counted on retaining much of the traffic of these districts for the Callander & Oban by steamer connection into the Ballachulish branch at Kentallen. As if to emphasise that a North Ballachulish line would feed the West Highland and not become part of a through route to Oban, the North British declared that a sufficient timetable could be contrived by utilising locomotives and rolling stock lying over at Fort William.

By 1912 (the experiment had begun some years earlier), MacBraynes had established a motor bus service between Fort William and North Ballachulish, connecting with the Callander & Oban trains at Ballachulish Ferry station. This required a quarter-mile walk on the south shore. Between the wars, the MacBrayne Company (from 1928 part-owned by the LMS) would move into road transport on a large scale. There were other signs of changing times. A 'motor car' was found to be an adequate substitute during 1912–13, when negotiations between the Invergarry & Fort Augustus and the North British were deadlocked, with the rail service withdrawn over many months. Moreover, the Caledonian contemplated using a similar vehicle between Ardgour and Loch Sunart (again with a Kentallen connection) in order to win back the mail contract for Moidart and Ardnamurchan, which had been captured for the West Highland route (and the Loch Shiel steamer) when the Mallaig Extension opened.

1. In association with Sir John Wolfe-Barry, of Tower Bridge fame, who advised as to the proposed sea-loch bridges (across Loch Etive, Loch Creran and Loch Leven).

Caledonian Railway.

CALLANDER AND OBAN LINE.

Opening Ceremony—Ballachulish Extension

On FRIDAY, 21st AUGUST, 1903.

SPECIAL TIME TABLE.

		a.m.
GLASGOW (Buchanan Street),	dep.	8.20
EDINBURGH (Princes Street) (Ordinary Train),	„	8.0
STIRLING,	„	9.0
DUNBLANE,	„	9.10
CALLANDER,	„	9.35
KILLIN JUNCTION,	„	10.18
DALMALLY,	„	11.10
CONNEL FERRY,	„	11.50
„ BRIDGE,	„	12.2p
CREAGAN BRIDGE,	„	12.37
BALLACHULISH,	arr.	1.30
„ by Coach,	dep.	1.35
For drive up Glencoe and return by Coaches to Hotel,		2.45

LUNCHEON IN BALLACHULISH HOTEL.

		p.m.
BALLACHULISH HOTEL by Coach,	dep.	3.40
KENTALLEN by Coach,	arr.	3.52
„ by Train,	dep.	3.55
CONNEL FERRY,	„	5.8
DALMALLY,	„	5.44
KILLIN JUNCTION,	„	6.41
CALLANDER,	„	7.23
DUNBLANE,	„	7.45
STIRLING,	„	7.54
EDINBURGH (Princes Street) (Ordinary Train),	arr.	9.27
GLASGOW (Buchanan Street),	„	8.40

Opening of the Callander & Oban Company's branch, 1903.

Filling the Ballachulish–Fort William gap – a MacBrayne bus, *c.* 1960, at Corran Ferry, where the proposed West Highland station would have tapped the districts westward from Ardgour. (Robert Grieves Collection, courtesy Sinclair)

Chapter Thirteen

OTHER MIGHT-HAVE-BEENS

Throughout the twentieth century the West Highland's 'missing links' – Ballachulish–Fort William and Fort Augustus–Inverness – occasioned vain regrets. Many hopes had been invested in the Light Railways Act of 1896, but the results were patchy. By 1914 it was clearly wishful thinking that motor bus and motor lorry could build up local traffic before a railway took over – on the contrary, they were competitors and their advance accelerated during the First World War. The Lloyd George Coalition's post-1918 Reconstruction programme embraced several gap-filling light railways, including a revived Spean-and-Spey line, but reconstruction was soon overtaken by retrenchment.

Of lesser-known schemes along the West Highland route, 1894–6 saw two examples which the North British would not countenance. A branch down the Roseneath peninsula from Garelochhead was briefly scouted. More persistent were the would-be promoters of a Whistlefield–Portincaple funicular (designed by Charles Forman) to connect with the Loch Goil piers by a dedicated steamer. The fishermen of Loch Long were enlisted, who preferred their traditional steamer link with Greenock. By carting to Arrochar & Tarbet station they lost the early markets on Clydeside; landing at Portincaple would relieve congestion in these narrow waters and shorten the rail journey.

While the Loch Fyne fishery sought rail access to Scotland's cities, the farmers of South Argyll wanted easier access to the markets of Stirling and Perth and to the wintering grounds of Strathmore and Moray, via the West Highland, the Crianlarich spur and the Callander & Oban. Connection with Inveraray had to be seriously considered when influential backers financed a preliminary survey, but the proposed branch, from Lochlomondside via Glen Kinglas, would be formidably expensive. The North British offered instead a light railway, under the new legislation of 1896, from Arrochar & Tarbet to St Catherine's on Loch Fyne, opposite Inveraray. It would have described a dramatic curve below The Cobbler, followed Glen Croe over the Rest-and-be-Thankful and terminated at the St Catherine's–Inveraray ferry.

The Caledonian Railway had long realised that 'residential' extension of the Glasgow–Helensburgh line to Garelochhead and Loch Long would make Arrochar a better railhead for Loch Fyne than Callander & Oban Dalmally. The Callander & Oban now parried the West Highland threat by bringing forward a Dalmally–Inveraray branch in their composite bill of 1896–7.[1] This the North British at once opposed. Though the rival parties both proclaimed their commitment, in hindsight the ensuing contest has an air of unreality – while the Dalmally–Inveraray line might become the anchor for a chain of light railways extending into Kintyre, the Arrochar–St Catherine's line might be extended to Strachur and Dunoon… North British and West Highland prevailed in that the Callander & Oban project was defeated, but the Loch Fyne Light Railway, duly authorised by the Board of Trade (as the 1896 Act provided), would never be begun.

The preamble to the West Highland Bill of 1888–9, while denying that the new line would rely excessively on tourists (as the Caledonian and the Highland alleged), nevertheless emphasised the continuing growth of summer traffic across the Highlands. Parliamentary witnesses found opportunity to enthuse over the possibility of a mountain railway for Ben Nevis, once the West Highland was open to Fort William. The Ben Nevis meteorological observatory and little 'hotel' were already something of a summer attraction, and the pony track that served them encouraged visitors to make the ascent. The summit building was linked by telegraph with a sea-level observatory at Fort William, with data coordinated. Begun in 1883, the project ended in 1904, after an unsuccessful appeal for government support. A preliminary survey was carried out in 1896–7 for a railway by Glen Nevis and the Nevis Gorge to Steall, thence climbing abruptly to the summit plateau, but nothing more resulted.

For such traffic, livestock and other, as could be found in the remote quarters of Breadalbane and Rannoch, the West Highland promoters promised railheads arguably more convenient than the Highland Railway's Aberfeldy and Pitlochry. Lucas & Aird's contract included a new road from Loch Rannoch to isolated Rannoch station (where earnings from passenger traffic would be greater than its bleak location suggests). Mooted but not pursued was a similar road from Glen Lyon by the Allt Lairg Mheuran to Gorton[2], or, more usefully, by Auch Glen to Bridge of Orchy.

1. This included improvements at Oban and extension (see Chapter Twelve) from Ballachulish Ferry to Ballachulish village.

2. As in Thomas Telford's proposed drove road from High Bridge (Spean Bridge) to Killin, surveyed at the beginning of the nineteenth century. By Glen Spean, Loch Treig and across Rannoch Moor, Charles Forman broadly followed Telford in laying out the West Highland.

Chapter Fourteen

FORT WILLIAM (1)

Since the 1970s, construction of the A82 bypass on the seawall where the railway once ran, together with redevelopment, has transformed the Fort William scene.

Entry to Fort William (Act of 1889) was along the River Lochy, through the crofting land (Black Parks) later occupied by North British Aluminium's 'company village' of Inverlochy. The line would have curved to the old fort by a causeway across the then estuary of the River Nevis. The deviation authorised in 1890 ran a little to the south-east, bridging the Nevis. It invaded (by prior agreement) Nevis Distillery, Belford Hospital and the Craigs cemetery, where reinterments and a retaining wall were required. Campbell of Monzie had purchased the fort when military use ceased but undertook to make the site available for a railway reaching Lochaber. His widow, Christina Cameron-Campbell of Callart, feudal superior of Fort William burgh, made this promise good, bequeathing the old fort to the West Highland Company.

The line continuing to the town pier – which required a stone-faced embankment along the shoreline – was presented as a tramway for light and intermittent use. By the 1890 Act it was extended (by a very small addition) across the pierhead to the distillery pier, which had become West Highland property. The town council, at that date styled 'police commissioners' welcomed the prospect of a seemly sea front:

> The Commissioners unanimously approve of the proposed Railway No. 6, provided that the same will be of the nature of a Tramway over an Esplanade, open to the Public, and that accesses will be given to the sea by steps, or otherwise, along the face of the Esplanade, with one or more boat slips.

But in 1893 the West Highland directors, now under the North British thumb, announced that their main line would be taken down the new sea wall, with the passenger station sited at right angles to the pierhead, blighting the town's expectations of a fine promenade with an unobtrusive tramway. The ensuing quarrel dragged on to 1896, with a truce for the West Highland opening in 1894 (see Chapter Eight). It was not impossible that the Board of Trade would order the removal of passenger accommodation to the old fort – in which event the opening day platform was to become a temporary station.

The eventual agreement, based on Major Marindin's 1894 report and scheduled to the West Highland Ballachulish Extension Act (which was otherwise a dead letter), prescribed boat slips and a footpath along the sea wall, with three access points across the track – at the platform ends, at the signal box and at the gated level crossing which gave entry to yard and shed. The Ballachulish line, if and when built (it never was), would be separated from the main road south by a stylish railing; it would have exited the town on a low viaduct, preserving access to the west-end beach[1] and to a new 'ornamental garden', for which the West Highland Company were bound to pay.

The pierhead station, once described as 'pompous' externally, had some oddities, including (until the 1950s) an iron 'turnpike' stair leading nowhere in particular; the cramped concourse had an attractive timbered roof. The layout was extremely tight; three platform roads merged into the single main, with just room enough to extend the original platforms a little. A fourth road, briefly contemplated, would have been little more than a holding bay for locomotives. From 1901 trains to and from Mallaig reversed at Fort William, with more 'topping and tailing'. Shunting out and in was regulated by the starter semaphores. The knowledgeable looked instead to the signal at the level crossing, a quarter-mile away, for a surer indication of departure. During the eight months of the winter timetable, bustle alternated with slumber, but the additional trains of June to September tested the station to the limit.

Well into the 1960s, Fort William's day was defined by the West Highland Sleeper. The following routine was typical, though not invariable, in the last winters of steam:

> The morning Glasgow–Mallaig, with the overnight 'London portion' in front, arrived into the seaside road. Double-headed, it overshot the station building, clearing the points at the station throat. Once uncoupled, the Eastfield engines drew forward, sometimes blocking the town pier. The relieving engine backed down, to perform any adding and subtracting at the tail; and the King's Cross vehicles (a brake-composite and two sleeping cars) were detached – to be shunted by the duty pilot, waiting in one of the bay roads, when the Mallaig coaches had departed. This released the Glasgow engines to the shed, where they were immediately turned and serviced. North British practice endured, and they would go south as they had arrived, with the assisting locomotive 'inside'. Each afternoon the Mallaig set returned, a comfortable fit for the seaside road; the engine, uncoupled, could draw clear without invading the pierhead. The 'inside' locomotive of the Eastfield pair backed down, attached any additional coaches, then shunted the entire rake on to the King's Cross three-some, which had been cleaned and prepared in the interval. The train engine appeared, to couple ahead, well outside the station, and the ensemble finally left for Glasgow, with the London set in the rear.

Today's station came into use in 1975, occupying what was already railway ground. The landward ramparts and dog-leg double gate of the old fort[2] had been levelled by Lucas & Aird some eighty years before and the area occupied by surfacemen's cottages and an untidy scatter of stores and workshops – one of them curiously dignified by a cat-and-mouse weather vane. All were now swept away. Freight facilities and locomotive servicing were first moved to the new depot at Tomnafaire, while the main line, altered to clear the new station site, still went down the shore to the old terminus, which grew increasingly shabby.

Today's layout is simple – a generous island serves two platform roads, one of them looped. On into the 1980s, locomotives were still changed, as a general rule, when Glasgow–Mallaig and Mallaig–Glasgow trains reversed, but the diesel-electric 27s and 37s ran round readily when necessary. Now Sprinters arrive, change direction and depart with a minimum of fuss. North of the station, diversion of the River Nevis has permitted redevelopment of An Aird. The West Highland Sleeper, which has survived precariously as an independent train, is stabled in an adjacent siding throughout the day, and other movements are unhindered. In summer these include the morning departure and afternoon return of the steam-hauled *Jacobite*. The Motorail service, for a few years usefully combined with the Sleeper, has been withdrawn.

1. Now covered by a large car park and the A82 bypass.

2. One of the old gates was re-erected at the entrance to the Craigs cemetery, where it still stands, just beyond today's station.

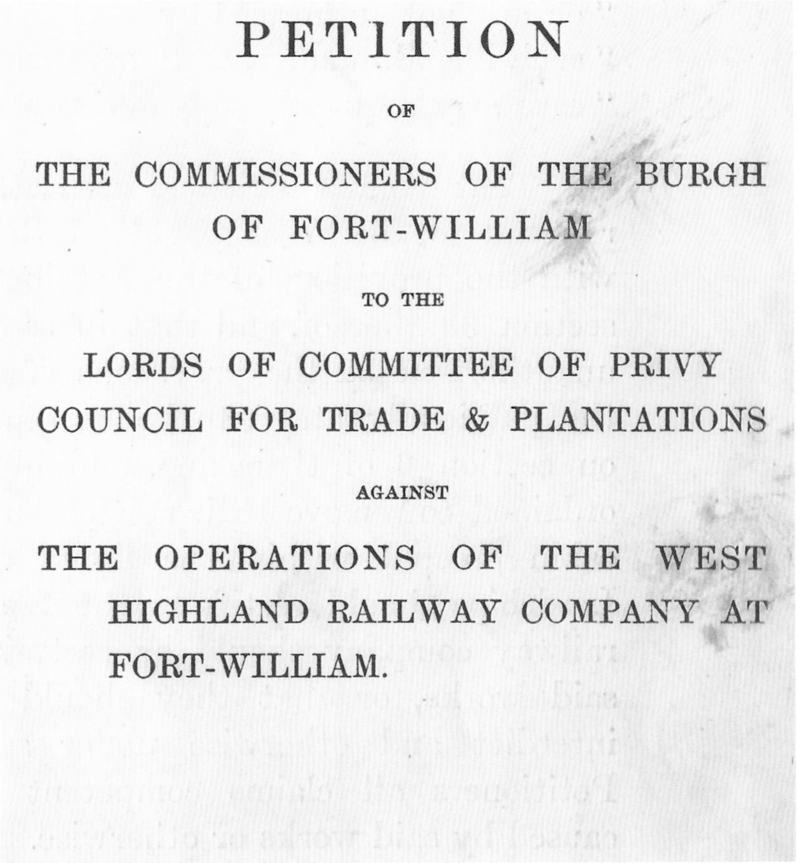

PETITION

OF

THE COMMISSIONERS OF THE BURGH OF FORT-WILLIAM

TO THE

LORDS OF COMMITTEE OF PRIVY COUNCIL FOR TRADE & PLANTATIONS

AGAINST

THE OPERATIONS OF THE WEST HIGHLAND RAILWAY COMPANY AT FORT-WILLIAM.

Appeal to the Board of Trade against railway occupation of the foreshore.

The seawall main line, Fort William, looking from the signal box to the gated level crossing and the old fort. The footpath (left) and the ungated crossing under the signalman's eye were public rights-of-way awarded by the Board of Trade. (SRPS)

NBR Class N (LNER Class D25) 4-4-0 603 (with 7-foot driving wheels, surely a very rare visitor to the steeply graded West Highland?), derailed at Fort William station throat in 1919. The constricted layout is obvious. (Hennigan Collection, courtesy of Lynn)

Having overshot the station, LNER /ex-NBR 9407 *Glen Beasdale* and 9307 *Glen Nevis* occupy the pierhead extension authorised in 1890. Both engines remain Westinghouse-fitted, their air pumps prominent. (Casserley)

'Black 5' 44996 has arrived from Glasgow; all three platforms are occupied, suggesting a summer afternoon *c.* 1960, and a K1 will take the train at platform 3 on to Mallaig. The through pierhead road (platform 1) is to the left. (Yuill)

A BRCW '27' heads the summer timetable Up Sleeper *c.* 1970. The limitations of the old station are again clear to see. The public footpath is to the right. (Stevenson)

In two-tone green and not yet a '27', BRCW Type 2 D5367 has brought a train into platform 1. The hotel in the background was built soon after the West Highland opened, meeting a growing tourist demand. (Robert Grieves Collection, courtesy Sinclair)

The last months of the old station, with the A82 bypass under construction. (Stevenson)

Seen from the yard in 1952, ex-North British 0-6-0 65300 shunts a rake of wagons – more or less where the new station now stands. Behind the engine are surfacemen's cottages, demolished in the redevelopment of the 1970s. (Casserley)

The yard and goods shed in North British days: electric lamps – one is prominent in the foreground – were installed by the Fort William Lighting Company, a pioneer of its kind. The skimpy loading bank (beside the crane) soon necessitated more generous provision, primarily for livestock, on the town side of the main line. (Alsop)

The new station nears completion. (Stevenson)

27 005 at the new station in June 1979: the retaining wall (middle distance) and the tracks to Nevis distillery (now replaced by modern housing) are vestiges of the West Highland entry to Fort William as once it was. (Noble)

The new station today: steam is matter-of-fact and the *Jacobite* continues well into autumn when the first snow sometimes dusts Ben Nevis. (Stone)

1990: 37 407 *Loch Long* shunts Motorail vans; development of An Aird has begun. (Noble)

Chapter Fifteen

FORT WILLIAM (2)

In the foreshore quarrel, it weakened the town's case that Fort William had invited the Glasgow & North Western engineer to bring his line along the water's edge, and North British high-handedness was excusable in that the old fort could not contain passenger, goods and locomotive facilities. Two barracks, already converted to dwellings and workshops, were retained as railwaymen's housing (supplemented by new tenements near the level crossing). The former barracks were not removed until the 1930s, when the LNER remodelled the layout and installed a modern turntable. The Tweeddale Place tenements (named for the marchioness who performed the opening ceremony in 1894) were demolished in the redevelopments of the 1970s.

The original stabling at Fort William was inadequate. Vans, wagons and even passenger stock were sometimes lodged in the sidings at Spean Bridge. Goods-handling at the old fort was improved by looping up two sidings and supplementing the skimpy loading bank with better facilities, primarily for livestock, on the opposite side of the main line. New sidings were inserted in the 'V' of Banavie Junction ('Mallaig Junction' from 1901). Initially lubricants and petrol were delivered in drums, as wagon traffic. BP tankers were subsequently accommodated at the Junction and Esso tankers at the old fort yard. Chapter Nineteen describes the expansion of goods traffic between the wars, when the LNER replaced the 'sea-side' goods shed with a 'town-side' building, fronting the livestock bank. Shunting the bank, and now the goods shed too, required possession of the sea-wall main, and was conducted between passenger movements; the points trailed in at the gated level crossing, from the 1930s remotely controlled.

Tablet regulations for the terminal section between Fort William and the junction allowed variation in workings. Certain goods trains departed from the yard loop, but others were propelled cautiously down the sea wall, to obtain their first token at the town box. Certain arrivals ran past the yard on the main, surrendered their last tablet, and reversed, again cautiously, into the loop. Add light engines to and from the station; add shunting at loading bank and goods shed; add (in summer) a passenger set for extension extras, taken to and from its siding at Mallaig Junction... There was altogether more activity along the sea wall, more openings and closings at the level crossing, than the public timetables showed. Locomotives backing down to the station waited, beyond the level crossing and in sight of the signalman, at the extreme end of the yard loop.

From the 1930s, when bulk alumina north of Burntisland and aluminium slab south of Falkirk became West Highland staples, the overnight Ghosts (see Chapter Nineteen) accounted for most of the freight traffic between Glasgow and Fort William. With the arrivals of the early morning divided up, that night's departures could be assembled. Engine movements in and out of the depot precluded systematic shunting of the open yard, and in later years this commenced after the morning passengers had come and gone and the Down goods for Mallaig had departed, when a lull fell on the locomotive shed. The yard pilot worked back and forth, in and out of the dead end which continued the loop, an unhurried performance – though butting loaded wagons up the incline to the coaling stage demanded a noisy burst of energy. During the Second World War the Mallaig Junction sidings were looped up and more sidings added. An incoming train could be pigeonholed there – and the Ghost devoted to alumina and aluminium empties usually was. The yard pilot, or one of its fellows, later tripped to the BA smelter and adjacent carbon plant.

The Fort William scene of the 1950s still included seasonal fish specials Up from Mallaig and fish 'empties' Down, which changed engines. There were occasional pilot trips along the Mallaig line to Annat (where the auction mart had been resited) or to Corpach (for ballast from Banavie quarry). Once or twice a week, a pilot shunted the sidings at Glenlochy distillery, just beyond the Nevis viaduct; Ben Nevis distillery, out beyond the smelter, received similar attention. Nevis distillery, oldest of the three, had ceased whisky production, but the bonded warehouses remained in use, made over to general storage. Here something of the old layout, with the Nevis sidings opening from the dead end, can still be grasped today, looking east from the new station.

Chapter Sixteen

CRIANLARICH

Roughly equidistant from Glasgow and Fort William, Crianlarich became (and has remained) an engineering and permanent way depot. After harsh experience in the West Highland's first winter, an engine shed and turntable were added. The platform 'dining room', a tight fit between station building and signalbox, emphasised Crianlarich's half-way status, as did the capacious water tank and duplicate columns. When double-headed trains crossed, the four engines could take water simultaneously.

Bridge of Orchy and Inverlair (Tulloch) were also candidates for 'refreshment rooms'. The former gave summer-season coach links (see Chapter Twenty-Nine). The latter, giving interchange with the regular coach to Kingussie, might have become the junction for a West Highland branch into Badenoch and Speyside (see Chapter Eleven). As can still be seen, the access road at Tulloch was laid out to provide a turning circle for the horse-drawn coach. But Crianlarich was the clear choice. The interval allowed each train was prominently displayed. Food baskets could be pre-ordered by telegraph – a facility appreciated by passengers in the through coach (not yet the West Highland Sleeper) from London. When, in 1901, Major Pringle RE came overnight to Spean Bridge for a first Board of Trade inspection of the Invergarry & Fort Augustus Railway, a fortifying breakfast basket was waiting for him at Crianlarich. From the 1920s, under LNER management, older coaching stock was phased out. The original West Highland vehicles of 1894 were 'state of the art' in their day, but lacked gangways; with all-corridor trains already the norm, restaurant cars could be introduced from 1929. Refreshment at Crianlarich became a more calculated exercise, with an eye to the signals and an ear for the guard's whistle, but the engines had to be watered still and the 'dining room' in café guise continued to prosper.

The Crianlarich spur did not open until 1897. An early plan shows the West Highland station positioned on the curve leading out across Strathfillan, the spur diverging at the Glasgow end; a stairway leads down to the Callander & Oban station, to be resited below. The Caledonian challenged the design of the viaduct over the Callander & Oban and next proposed (for delay's sake) an expensive joint station on the east bank of Fillan Water, laid out to allow through running both Craigendoran-to-Oban and Callander-to-Fort William. Arbitration finally disposed of Caledonian objections to the spur itself, but the Board of Trade award necessitated purchase of an additional parcel of land. This, along with disputed water rights, gave the local proprietor a lever. As owner of Crianlarich Hotel, he resisted the station 'dining room'.

Denied running powers to Oban, the North British became indifferent to exchange of traffic and suspicious of Caledonian machinations. A Caledonian claim for running powers to Fort William, whether onwards from Crianlarich or via Ballachulish, would delay, perhaps frustrate, the West Highland Mallaig Extension, which the North British were determined to share with no one. (The mischief-making Caledonian argued for maximum use by all comers of a state-assisted railway – see Chapter Twelve). A pilot at Crianlarich to work the spur, additional to the ballast and snow-plough engine stabled there, was unnecessary, but the Caledonian dragged out the negotiations whereby the locomotives of both companies' regular goods trains eventually handled transfers as required. The North British for their part were in no hurry. Pressure to reach agreement came from John Anderson, secretary-manager of the Callander & Oban, who counted on a modest but useful exchange of traffic.

Passenger trains on the Crianlarich spur (other than excursions) were for a long time limited to a summer-only return service between Glasgow Queen Street and Oban, initiated by the LNER and LMS and reintroduced under British Railways. From 1966, with the eastern half of the Callander & Oban closed and Oban trains running via Helensburgh, West Highland Crianlarich came to seem very much a junction. 'Winter' passenger provision spread across the day, there being three 'Obans' in each direction as well as the traditional Glasgow–Mallaig and Mallaig–Glasgow trains. Passenger services still began with the Down West Highland Sleeper around 8 a.m., but now ended with the evening Glasgow–Oban around 8.30 p.m. Though the timetable saw several adjustments over the ensuing twenty years, there was no attempt to combine Oban services with those to and from Fort William and Mallaig – until in 1989 locomotive haulage ceased (save for the sleeper). Sprinters now divide and unite at Crianlarich, a subdued performance by comparison with the fire-cleaning and watering of steam days, but there is time, as ever, to patronise the quondam 'dining room'.

A pair of BR/ex-LNER Class B1 4-6-0s, southbound, take water at Crianlarich in the early 1950s, when lower-quadrant signals still characterised the West Highland. The leading engine is 61243 *Sir Harold Mitchell.* (Casserley)

A vigorous restart – BR Standard 5 4-6-0 7307 and K2 pilot (conventionally 'inside'), head a 1950s Glasgow–Mallaig out of Crianlarich. (Naional Railway Museum/Science & Society Picture Library)

A 1950s special working via the Crianlarich spur approaches the upper junction: a nameless K2 leads a B1. (Stevenson)

A timber train leaves Crianlarich for Annat pulp and paper mill, *c.* 1970, behind 27 043. The viaduct spans the Callander & Oban line, now abandoned eastwards. (Noble)

27 001 rests at Crianlarich (June 1986). (Noble)

The so-called *Lord of the Isles*. Photographers and film crews occasionally require a masquerade. (Johnstone)

'Black 5' 45231 *The Sherwood Forrester* and K1 62005 head the northbound *Jacobite* stock in May 2009. The 2-6-0 is 'disguised' as *Lord of the Isles* (the name once carried by BR/ex-LNER K4 61996). To the left are Crianlarich's platform café and the station building, which has replaced the original 'chalet'. (Henshaw)

An Oban Sprinter awaits its Mallaig-and-Fort William partner. The engine shed (1895) is now an engineering workshop, but Crianlarich's turntable has been removed. (Furnevel)

Splitting Sprinters. (Crawford)

FAST DIESEL SERVICE

BETWEEN

GLASGOW (Queen Street) and OBAN

MONDAYS TO FRIDAYS

GLASGOW (Queen Street)	depart	9 35 am
CRAIGENDORAN	,,	10 10 am
CRIANLARICH UPPER	arrive	11 20 am
LOCH AWE	,,	11 57 am
CONNEL FERRY	,,	12 31 pm
OBAN	,,	12 50 pm

Does not convey Glasgow to Craigendoran passengers.

OBAN	depart	5 15 pm
CONNEL FERRY	,,	5 29 pm
LOCH AWE	,,	6 2 pm
CRIANLARICH UPPER	,,	6 41 pm
CRAIGENDORAN	arrive	7 48 pm
GLASGOW (Queen Street)	,,	8 30 pm

Does not convey Craigendoran to Glasgow passengers.

Seats may be reserved in advance from Glasgow (Queen Street) and Oban

Miniature Buffet Car for light refreshments

Long before 'Beeching', the LMS and LNER introduced a summer service between Glasgow Queen Street and Oban, via Helensburgh and the Crianlarich spur. It was revived under British Railways, latterly employing a 3-car DMU with buffet counter.

Chapter Seventeen

SOUTHERN END

The promoters of the Glasgow & North Western Railway had counted on residential development in the direction of Strathendrick and Loch Lomond. The West Highland Company hoped to encourage outer-suburban traffic along the Gare Loch. As first envisaged, Fort William trains were to be 'express' between Glasgow and Garelochhead: they would coordinate there with 'semi-fasts', serving Craigendoran, Helensburgh Upper (where commuters were cossetted with the covered entry ramp which still survives today), Rhu and Shandon.[1]

On the hillside where the West Highland ran, house-building advanced slowly. The established communities along the shore found the steamers sufficiently convenient, and the Queen Street–Garelochhead trains were soon replaced by a Craigendoran–Arrochar all-stations shuttle, connecting with the long-established Glasgow–Helensburgh service.[2] Though the turntable at Garelochhead was retained, pending further experience, the new arrangement became permanent. This mollified the Colquhoun Trustees, who wanted better facilities for Lochlongside and insisted on a station for Whistlefield – a commitment which North British and West Highland had tried to evade. A platform and basic building, in modified 'chalet' style, plus a siding, were provided in 1896. The shuttle also gave a limited passenger service at Glen Douglas passing place, where the Colquhouns' tenant farmers had already petitioned successfully for a siding and loading bank.

The Shandon Hydropathic Company were eager for rail connection – their managing director, James Morrison, was a named West Highland promoter, and he thought the first timetable a betrayal. Shandon's visitors from further afield were obliged to change into the local train at Glasgow; their residents seeking a day trip along the new railway faced a change at Garelochhead. In the event, Fort William trains soon became 'all stations' north from Craigendoran, or called conditionally at Shandon, additional to the shuttle. During the First World War the Hydro was requisitioned by the Admiralty. Afterwards, the North British refused to acquire the struggling business.

Despite the fiction of West Highland independence, finally dropped from 1908, the line south of Ardlui was always managed from Glasgow. The Arrochar local service was oriented to the city, and the West Highland from the first was included in the Clyde Coast and Loch Lomond timetables, which expanded in the tourist season to feature elaborate 'circular' permutations by rail, road and water. Summer traffic meant additional trains to Arrochar & Tarbet or Ardlui, especially at weekends. As long as steam lasted, the summer sheets showed a Saturday afternoon return working – it ran on to Crianlarich, where the engine was turned and serviced. And the short-lived diesel replacement still extended to Ardlui on summer weekends.

1. The designations were originally 'Upper Helensburgh' and 'Row'.
2. The original Helensburgh terminus became Helensburgh Central.

'Push-pull' C15 4-4-2T 67460 propels the Arrochar & Tarbet shuttle out of Helensburgh Upper. A Mallaig–Glasgow occupies the Up road; BR's early carmine-and-cream did not flatter ex-LNER stock. (Casserley)

An Up DMU enters Garelochhead in the final years of the Arrochar & Tarbet locals. (Stevenson)

Rhu, looking south, reduced (for a second time) to single track. The loop, removed in the 1920s, was restored during the Second World War. (Stevenson)

Shandon under snow: Garelochside and Lochlongside are sometimes snow-clad when the line further north escapes. (Stevenson)

Whistlefield, looking north. (Stevenson)

Combined cottage and signal box between the running lines at Glen Douglas. A little gardening is in evidence. (Stevenson)

A BR/ex-LNER V1 2-6-2T with a three-coach train enters Arrochar & Tarbet from Ardlui. (Stevenson)

Chapter Eighteen

THE WEST HIGHLAND SLEEPER

The West Highland promoters promised a cross-Border service by the East Coast route. Initially a single composite coach between London Kings Cross and Fort William, this gratified others besides the Shandon Hydropathic Company. 1895, which saw the West Highland's first full summer, also saw the celebrated 'Race to Aberdeen', East Coast against West Coast (respectively the Great Northern, North Eastern and North British companies and the London & North Western and Caledonian companies). In the mid-August working timetables, the 'Racer', for Dundee and Aberdeen, was followed out of Kings Cross by the complementary 8.10 p.m.: 'Consists of vehicles for Edinburgh, Glasgow and the Highland Railway, and for Oban when necessary.[1] West Highland traffic and the through carriage for Fort William will also be sent by this train.'

When the West Highland Extension opened (1901), through vehicles between London and Mallaig featured in the summer timetable – it proved a short-lived experiment. Also a partner in the Midland Route to Scotland, the North British handled the Midland Company's traffic for Edinburgh, Aberdeen and Inverness,[2] and, in several summers before 1914, through coaches were run overnight between London St Pancras and Fort William, going circuitously by Carlisle and Edinburgh. Eventually, the West Highland 'London portion' by the East Coast would run year-round. In late LNER and then BR practice, three vehicles made up the usual winter sets – a first-class sleeper, a third- (second from 1960) class sleeper and a compartment composite brake.[3] These left London in the rear of the 'Aberdonian' (with a catering vehicle at the absolute tail, detached at York). Shunted at Edinburgh Waverley in the very small hours, they were taken forward by a following train (the overnight Colchester–Glasgow) then shunted again at Queen Street, to head the morning Glasgow–Mallaig. Beyond Garelochhead, around 7 a.m., the gangway doors were unlocked for access to breakfast in the restaurant car.

In summer the 'London portion' expanded; again, LNER practice continued beyond nationalisation. The London–Fort William vehicles were included in an East Coast 'overnight', to unite with a very early West Highland service out of Edinburgh, independent of the morning Glasgow–Mallaig. Taking the East Junction–North Junction chord at Cowlairs, the combined train avoided reversal in and out of Queen Street and might better by two hours the winter arrival into Fort William. In the June–September timetable of 1964, the 3.35 a.m. from Edinburgh (7.30 p.m. ex Kings Cross the previous evening) reached Fort William at 8.20 a.m.; on Saturdays (Friday evening ex Kings Cross), a 'relief' brought more London vehicles north, and the Edinburgh–Fort William, thus lengthier and running ten minutes later, included a restaurant car.

Though double-heading, most frequent in summer, was to be expected at weekends and holiday periods throughout the West Highland year, only the sleeper offered a daily performance during the eight months' currency of the winter timetable. In the mid-1950s the regular pairing, out and back from Glasgow Eastfield, was a Black 5 4-6-0 and a K2 2-6-0 pilot, the latter coupled inside the train engine, North British fashion. As they backed up Fort William sea wall to the shed at journey's end, their combined whistles – LMS hoot and LNER shriek – gave unmistakable notice to the waiting town. How much the day turned on this train is now difficult to recall. Along with 'English newspapers',[4] it brought 'English mail' for the second postal delivery. Weddings were timed for its afternoon departure, when the guests and inevitable piper took over the station, to speed bride and groom on their way. More sombrely, the city exile attending a Lochaber funeral also relied on the sleeper, making the round trip from Edinburgh or Glasgow. In the first diesel days the winter service was still double-headed, and Eastfield's preferred Type 2 partners were a 'Birmingham Sulzer' (BRCW) and an English Electric 'single-cab'. The latter, slighter locomotive ran 'inside', and Fort William reshuffled the pair so that they went south in the same order – which, superficially at least, preserved tradition for a little longer.

From the 1970s Anglo-Scottish overnight services were concentrated at Euston. Over the West Highland, the 'London portion' was still combined, to and from Fort William, with the morning Glasgow–Mallaig and the afternoon Mallaig–Glasgow; but arrangements varied – e.g. for some years the southbound train paused at remodelled Cowlairs, where the sleeping cars and brake composite were detached. The BRCW Type 2s (Class 27), which had proved capable of taking, single-handedly, the usual seven or eight vehicles, were superseded in the 1980s by EE Class 37s – steam-heated like the 27s. The new generation of sleeping cars had electric heat, and the short-term answer was conversion of three redundant Class 25s to ETHEL units.

Of West Coast and Caledonian Railway ancestry, the London–Oban overnight service disappeared 'post-Beeching'. Connection in and out of the West Highland Sleeper at Crianlarich remained unsatisfactory. It has been urged more than once that Oban makes a better destination for through passengers between London and the western Highlands. But today the sleeper still terminates at Fort William – as an independent service, both summer and winter. Sprinters have operated to Fort William, Mallaig and Oban since 1989: the sleeper, if it runs at all, must run alone, and the service has survived precariously. Patronage was for a time reinforced by adding a Motorail service, now discontinued. Passengers in the seated accommodation must change at Edinburgh.

1. From the 1860s parliament tried to balance railway interests within Scotland, Caledonian and North British, West Coast and East Coast. The Caledonian did not encourage, but were bound to entertain, 'enemy' traffic over the Callander & Oban line.
2. The Glasgow & South Western Railway provided the Midland Company's link with Glasgow.
3. Third-class sleeping accommodation came late to Britain's railways – a welcome improvement of the inter-war years.
4. The Ghost goods carried Scottish newspapers (see Chapter Nineteen).

Traditional Sleeper – van; London set; Glasgow–Mallaig set (with buffet-restaurant car) – arriving northbound into Crianlarich in August 1974. (Noble)

Minimal Sleeper, 1990s – the Down service nears County March in a chilly November dawn. (Henshaw)

The Down Sleeper approaches Cruach snow-shed (2010). (Crawford)

Through the rainbow to Corrour – patchy snow lingers as the sun rises on Rannoch Moor. (Fielding)

The traditional ensemble, on the long descent into Glen Spean, approaches the Treig tunnel. (Stone)

The Up Sleeper rounds Monessie Gorge in August 2008; the River Spean, depleted since the 1930s by the Lochaber Power Scheme, can still run high after rain (cf. p.121 lower right). (Henshaw)

Summer-evening – the Up Sleeper climbs towards Auchindaul below the Ben Nevis cliffs, in 2010. (Henshaw)

Fort William – new station but traditional Sleeper arrival (1979). (Stone)

Chapter Nineteen

TRADITIONAL GOODS AND MODERN FREIGHT

With Roshven disallowed, there were fears for the West Highland Bill in the second house[1] (see Chapter Nine). The disadvantaged communities of the west coast and the Islands would gain little from a railway terminating at Fort William. That the line would eventually serve them and professionalise the crofter-fishermen remained a plausible claim, but one yet to be made good. The Highland Company and the Callander & Oban warned that their loadings at Strome Ferry and Oban were hard-won, in competition with the fishery steamers running direct from the west coast both to the Clyde and to Lancashire.

Fort William's two distilleries (a third would be added) were the largest immediate source of railway income, and the deviated line gave sidings to all three. Distiller D. P. MacDonald dispensed with his steamer and sold his pier (accessed by the short extension authorised in 1890) to the West Highland Company (see Chapter Fourteen). Though a West Highland promoter, MacDonald would have settled, like the Lochaber landowners, for rail connection with Connel Ferry. For years past, the Caledonian had brought his Mearns barley to Oban. He was also a substantial farmer, with holdings on Lord Abinger's Inverlochy estate – a reminder that the backers of the West Highland Railway cannot be neatly boxed by interest, profession or social class.

It is a comment on the all-too-optimistic forecasts which accompanied the West Highland promotion that MacDonald did not expect his transport costs to be much reduced. The benefits were a regular, reliable service and the convenience of wagon-load as against ship-load. There was coal traffic to be won all along the route but in the Gareloch and Loch Long, and at Fort William, the sea remained a competitor.[2] Lanarkshire coal came cheaper by the West Highland to Crianlarich and Tyndrum, and Caledonian charges, via Stirling and Callander, were correspondingly reduced. (The shorter route set the rate, under Clearing House inter-company agreements.) Mature timber provided an erratic return traffic, but the established trade in thinnings – some of which became reels and spools for the Paisley thread industry – remained with the coastal lighters.

Fishing at Fort William was declining. The Loch Long fishery would remain active but consignments in later years were modest, often conveyed in passenger brake-vans. From 1901, when the Mallaig Extension opened, seasonal fish specials Up (and fish 'empties' Down) were a familiar feature of the West Highland, and it became the practice at any time to attach a few fish vans to the Mallaig–Glasgow passenger trains – which complicated remarshalling at Fort William and reception into Queen Street. Livestock was a more regular business. Despite claiming that the West Highland could find (or create) its own traffic, without harming the Highland Railway or the Callander & Oban, the promoters meant to intercept at Bridge of Orchy droves heading for Callander & Oban Tyndrum, and to divert from Highland Dalwhinnie to Spean Bridge those crossing from the Great Glen by the Corryarack. Fort William obtained a new auction mart at Nevis Bridge. On sale days, sheep and cattle were herded to the railway yard; a loop with loading bank and pens, on the town side of the main line, was an early and urgent addition to the layout (see Chapter Fifteen).

On into the new century, a daily train in each direction, serving the entire route, was usually sufficient for general goods, with some additional workings between Glasgow and Crianlarich. West Highland gradients entailed strict regulation at intermediate stations and passing places; certain sidings became 'one direction', which might add a day in transit, with consignments worked to the next station and brought back. In 1947, after twenty years of LNER ownership, all the old rules remained, for example:

• Glen Douglas siding must be shunted by Down trains only and no shunting must be done on the main line unless the engine is at the Arrochar & Tarbet end of the wagons.
• No portion of a Down train must be left outside the Home signal at Tyndrum during shunting operations. Before the engine is uncoupled the points must be set for the dead-end siding.
• The spring catch points on the Up loop at Roy Bridge are trailing to Up trains, and guards must see that the points are set in the running position during shunting along the loop in the facing direction.

Goods traffic on the West Highland was transformed during the 1920s and 1930s by the establishment of aluminium smelting at Fort William, as the adjunct of the Lochaber power scheme. The North British Aluminium Company's new plant was on a larger scale than their pioneering smelters at Foyers and Kinlochleven.[3] For the hydro-electric works, Loch Treig became a holding reservoir, fed from Loch Laggan (and ultimately from the head waters of the Spey). This necessitated a 1½-mile deviation, including a tunnel, past the Treig dam. During construction, Fersit ballast siding, at the foot of Loch Treig, grew into a depot and temporary passenger halt. When the smelter was commissioned, there were daily 'BA' consignments – alumina (refined from bauxite at Burntisland) north to Fort William and aluminium south to Falkirk rolling mill, with balancing empties. Overnight goods workings in both directions were introduced, known to railwaymen (and to Fort William at large) as the Ghosts. The town grew, and Inverlochy, North British Aluminium's 'company village' (near Mallaig Junction), added to the local population. Thus year-round passenger business increased, while summer traffic assumed new dimensions (see Chapter Twenty-Nine).

The Second World War put the West Highland under great pressure. LNER working timetables show how Ghost workings multiplied, with additional goods trains by day. Military and naval personnel were regular travellers. Spean Bridge became the railhead for the Commando centre at Achnacarry. Along the extension there were naval establishments at Corpach and Annat, and special services took over Inverailort House. An emergency harbour, rail-connected, was created at Faslane bay on the Gare Loch, against the threat of bombing on the upper Clyde, with the new Faslane Junction between Rhu and Shandon. (For training specialist units before the Normandy landings, Continental signalling equipment was installed on the Faslane branch.) Additional sidings were installed at Mallaig Junction and the existing sidings were looped up. The loop at Helensburgh Upper was lengthened, to accommodate Faslane traffic. Reduced since 1933 to a weekly coal train, the moribund Invergarry & Fort Augustus was designated an emergency route to the North and experienced a new lease of life, as Great Glen timber was hastily harvested. Post-1945, the West Highland gained a passing place at Inveruglas (since removed) and a temporary halt in Glen Falloch, both serving the Loch Sloy hydroelectric scheme. Unrepatriated prisoners of war were employed, travelling daily from Faslane Junction (where the remains of the wooden platform can still be identified today).

1. The West Highland Bill of 1888–9 began in the House of Lords then proceeded to the Commons.
2. The author's grandfather ran a coal and oil business from Fort William railway yard. Sea competition ensured that he was excused demurrage.
3. The NBA Company was among the initial backers of the Invergarry & Fort Augustus Railway, in the hope of a Fort Augustus-Inverness line through Foyers (Loch Ness) – site of their pioneering 1890s plant. Their Kinlochleven smelter was rail-served via the Callander & Oban Ballachulish branch, the final link being first by water and later by road.

Advertisement for D. P. MacDonald's whisky, with a fanciful representation of rail-connected Ben Nevis Distillery, Lochy Bridge, which he leased from Lord Abinger. Both were promoters of the West Highland Railway. (Stevenson)

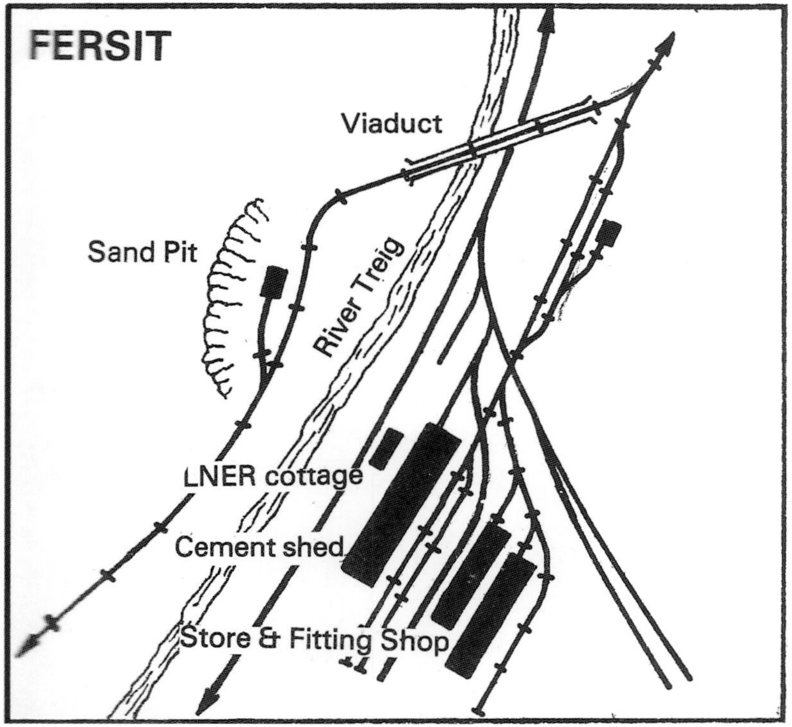

During construction of the Lochaber Power Scheme and North British Aluminium's Lochaber smelter, Fersit ballast siding at the foot of Loch Treig expanded into an exchange depot, with a temporary passenger platform. Contractor Balfour Beattie's narrow gauge system (shown hatched) reached from Fort William to Loch Laggan. (Late Patrick Howat) See also p.88 lower left.

Second World War – the 'secret port' at Faslane.

LNER successor to the 'native' North British 0-6-0s: Class J39 2738 heads an Up train south of Arrochar. From the 1940s 4-6-0s would increasingly take over. (Yuill)

A BRCW Sulzer in original condition (two-tone green, white window surrounds, no garish yellow warning panels) shunts at Ardlui, where an Up passenger is expected. (Stevenson)

BR/ex-LMS 'Black 5' 44707 on an Up working at Crianlarich, where a Down passenger has priority. The engine mounts a buffer-beam snow plough. Empty alumina hoppers are marshalled to the rear of the train. (Stevenson)

With Ben Dorain sharply defined ahead, another Sulzer (in rail-blue and officially a '27') climbs from Tyndrum to County March. (Noble)

37 404 *Ben Cruachan* climbs into Strathtulla with a Down alumina-cum-aluminium slab 'empties'. Imagine, in the background, the Glasgow & North Western Railway, tracing the edge of Blackmount. (Henshaw)

A Class 08 shunter, successor to Fort William's long-serving 0-6-0 pilots, shunts slab 'empties' at Lochaber smelter. (Henshaw)

Chapter Twenty

CROSSINGS

Radio control (Railway Electric Token Block) has replaced traditional signalling on the single-track West Highland, but the underlying principle – sole occupancy of a tablet section – endures. Craigendoran (West Highland), Helensburgh Upper, Rhu, Shandon, Garelochhead, Arrochar & Tarbet, Ardlui, Crianlarich, Tyndrum (subsequently Tyndrum Upper/Upper Tyndrum), Bridge of Orchy, Rannoch, Tulloch, Roy Bridge and Spean Bridge all had crossing loops, conventionally aligned for left-hand running. The longest sections (Garelochhead–Arrochar & Tarbet, Bridge of Orchy–Rannoch and Rannoch–Tulloch) were divided by additional passing places – Glen Douglas, Gorton and Corrour. Glen Douglas would graduate to local halt, and Corrour would become fully public. North British enginemen trusted the quick-acting Westinghouse brake, and a brisk approach to intermediate stations became characteristic of the line through all the years of steam – unless a crossing was scheduled. Tablet exchange was always dextrous. The winter passenger service was 'all stations' (as near as made no difference), and the general goods shunted all along the route, but excursions, limited goods and summer 'reliefs' took the loops where no stop was required at best speed, with small concession to the firemen and signalmen, who in one action caught and released the tablet pouches.

After 1918 working hours were more closely regulated, with lodging turns reduced: drivers, firemen and guards changed over when their train crossed the working which balanced their own. An entirely symmetrical timetable was impossible; moreover, shifts were complicated by double-heading. And the public sheets do not tell the whole story. In working timetables and weekly traffic notices, ballast and engineering trains were (and are) arranged so that passenger services can pass with the least hindrance.

From Craigendoran (West Highland) to Rannoch, all the stations were island – save side-platform Rhu, squeezed in a cutting. The three stations in Glen Spean were also side-platform – Tulloch, Roy Bridge and Spean Bridge. Signalling at Craigendoran Junction would be modified over the years. North from Helensburgh, dwarf signal cabins were standard, in harmony with the low-set, chalet-style station buildings. These cabins contained lever frame and indicators, while the tablet equipment was secured within the stationmaster's office – a separation which at first perturbed the railway inspectorate. Helensburgh Upper would acquire a taller box during the Second World War, to command the lengthened loop and additional sidings. At Rhu sighting from the outset required a higher structure but Rhu's loop would be removed, restored and removed again. Crianlarich had (and still has, out of use) what might be called a cut-down North British box at the north end of the platform, looking to the spur. Conventional boxes stood within the loops at Glen Douglas, Gorton and Corrour; at Banavie Junction (Mallaig Junction from 1901); and at Fort William. When Spean Bridge became a junction, accommodating the Invergarry & Fort Augustus Railway, the original cabin was altered; after fire damage, it would be replaced by the LNER.

After 1901 the West Highland's slender winter timetable was largely fixed by steamer connections at Mallaig, by the overnight London–Fort William service, and by the inflexible requirements of the GPO. One passenger 'meet' became an institution – at Spean Bridge, where the morning Glasgow–Mallaig/London–Fort William crossed the morning Mallaig–Glasgow. The Invergarry & Fort Augustus branch train gave connection into both services – and connection back to Fort Augustus. When in 1933 passenger service on the Fort Augustus line ceased, MacBrayne buses provided the Great Glen link, which remained a postal link too. Ardlui was for long the other regular rendezvous, where the afternoon Mallaig–Glasgow, combining at Fort William with the Up London service, met the evening Glasgow–Mallaig.

Summer on the West Highland in the 1950s meant through coaches from Edinburgh, with more shunting at Fort William and Mallaig to make up the return sets, besides additional trains on the extension. But the provision was essentially an extra train in each direction – a mid-morning Glasgow–Mallaig; a second Up service in the afternoon, giving a later London departure from Fort William. And this meant unbalanced workings and complex rosters for enginemen and guards. On summer weekends (in some seasons every weekday) the 'London portion' added Edinburgh–Mallaig coaches and formed an independent train, without reversal in Glasgow (see Chapter Eighteen). Duplicate services were a weekend 'must'. In the summer timetable of 1957, for example, the 6.40 a.m. Saturday Up 'relief' met a cavalcade of Down trains – the overnight ex. London-and-Edinburgh at Spean Bridge; the 'relief' Glasgow–Mallaig (limited stop) at Roy Bridge; the all-stops Glasgow–Mallaig at Tulloch; and the 3.45 p.m. Glasgow–Mallaig had four Saturday crossings – it met the midday 'relief' ex-Mallaig at Arrochar & Tarbet; the principal afternoon Up train at Ardlui; the second 'relief' at Bridge of Orchy; the Edinburgh-and-London at Gorton …

Mallaig Junction had no loop in the direction of Spean Bridge; but a crossing could be contrived on summer mornings by holding the Up Glasgow service (after reversal in Fort William) 'wrong road' in the extension loop. An extension 'extra' overtook 'right road', and the Down train ex. Glasgow arrived, whereupon the Mallaig–Glasgow could reverse, to resume its interrupted journey. Also prescribed was a 'meet' in Fort William's cramped station, where the first afternoon service up from Mallaig and the mid-morning ex-Glasgow both changed engines and reversed, while the one acquired additional vehicles and the other shed its observation car.

The double-headed trains of June to September entered each passing station with deliberation – and little room to spare. With the points reversed for passage in the opposite direction, the crossing service could come in more boldly. Under the stationmaster's eye, enginemen and guards compared notes and changed from train to train. It was an occasion sometimes protracted – by an ailing locomotive, by timetable exigencies, or by dealing with an out-of-the-ordinary consignment. Yet, measured against a long summer day, the interlude was fleeting; when the two services had gone their separate ways and all sound had faded, the lonely station was lonely once more. Winter evening 'meets' were different. Though open coaches were employed in summer, and might be added at any season for weekend traffic, compartment stock made up the regular winter sets. Enclosed amid the rolling darkness, travellers felt the brakes come on, altering the rhythm of the wheels. Then hazy lamplight appeared – made all the hazier by the condensation inseparable from steam-heat. As engine and then coaches took the points, firebox glow and a string of windows, with the whiter quality of electric light, defined the train waiting in the other road. Muffled voices, slamming doors, a flash of green from the guard's hand lamp, an emphatic whistle – and darkness resumed as the station slid away.

Glen Douglas: BR Class 6 72001 *Clan Cameron*, heading the Clan Cameron Rally special in June 1956, meets an Up local. (Stevenson)

Arrochar & Tarbet, 1972: Sulzer meets Sulzer. The 1970s belonged to the BRCWs; 'D' prefixes disappeared when steam ended, while green (right) gave way to blue (left). (Noble)

In the first diesel winters, southbound Sleeper and evening Glasgow–Mallaig met at Crianlarich – and so (summer timetable) did the early Mallaig–Glasgow and the mid-morning Down extra: enginemen and guards changed over. (Furnevel)

Crianlarich, twenty-five years later – Sprinter meets *Loch Long*, heading oil empties. (Henshaw)

November 1984: at 1,300 feet above sea level, the morning Mallaig–Glasgow runs into Corrour: on the waiting Down Sleeper an ETHEL (Electric Train Heating Ex-Locomotive) is coupled inside the train engine. (Noble)

Chapter Twenty-One

MAINTENANCE, RAILWAYMEN AND SNOW

Following the wash-out in Strathtulla in July 1889 (see Chapter Eight), Major Marindin's made the succinct comment that 'the West Highland line would need a lot of watching'. In the final push to completion, no provision had been made for resident surfacemen. Contractor and engineer conventionally assumed responsibility for maintenance during a new railway's first year; and during the early months of traffic, as consolidation and ballasting work continued, routine attention to the track became another task for Lucas & Aird's men, travelling daily from Craigendoran, Crianlarich and Fort William. However, with other work of all kinds outstanding, this basic duty was haphazardly performed. Alerted by the complaints of engine drivers (who risked running down careless squads without warning flags or lamps) and fearful of Board of Trade intervention, the North British took over comprehensively from October 1894, when the ballast squads transferred to railway employment.

There were station buildings unfinished, loading banks without a top surface or livestock pens, sidings without buffer stops... Taxed with these deficiencies, engineer Charles Forman retorted that the North British were themselves to blame, having insisted that everything inessential be postponed so as to have the line open for traffic that summer. He also warned that the North British, in settling with the sub-contractors, would face more delay – and so it proved. Some hasty remedies could be found – blinding the banks with ash placated the farmers whose sheep had suffered injury, but surfacemen's houses, spaced along the route walking-length by walking-length, were now all-important. Wooden dwellings were ordered pending completion of permanent cottages (Some of the latter, variously altered or left to decay, can still be seen).

The North British engineer's department took almost two years to eliminate the general backlog. Last in the queue were stationmasters and other staff at intermediate stations, whose houses lay in various stages of completion. In the autumn of 1895 the traffic department warned, and no wonder, of discontent: with a second winter approaching, 'the Signalman at Rannoch, the Signalman and his wife and daughter at Spean Bridge, and the Signalman at Tulloch are still living in Waiting Rooms, and the Signalman at Crianlarich in a wooden hut'. In the previous December, as New Year 1895 approached, life on the high moorland had brought the Corrour signalman to despair: 'It is impossible to keep the instruments in working order; as there is no porch, rain pours in at the door. I am standing in three inches of water. This is the last complaint I shall make. Part of the roof was blown off today.'

Winters during construction were, for the most part, wild and wet, but that of 1894/5 turned arctic over much of Scotland, and the West Highland was three times blocked for several days:

> The drifting was very heavy and rapid and the cuttings along the line were speedily choked. The worst parts were:- two miles on either side of Tulloch station, the wreath (drift) being 8-15 feet deep; between the top of Loch Treig and Corrour; and Cruach cutting which was perfectly solid from end to end, on the high side about 30 feet deep.
>
> William Arnott, NBR district superintendent, Fort William, 11 January 1895.

There being no turntable between Garelochhead and Fort William and no water for locomotives between Bridge of Orchy and Tulloch, snow ploughing was severely hampered. No means of opening up the line at night was as yet available after the last scheduled trains had passed.

Emergency call-out circuits, integrated with the tablet equipment, were installed in all the stationmasters' houses: seventy years later, this system was unchanged in principle. An engine shed and turntable were installed at Crianlarich and a turntable at Rannoch (where the remains of the pit and siding can still be traced). Rannoch also acquired water columns: the feeder tank, though improvised from an old engine-boiler, gave long service. Dwarf walls and an overall roof, in longitudinal sections, were added to the raw rock of Cruach cutting to create a unique snowshed: the centre section was removed each summer, lessening the wear and tear from exhaust blast. In the winters ahead, locomotives on the West Highland would be fitted with buffer-beam snow ploughs to overcome minor drifting. These did not hamper double-heading and often remained in place well into summer. Snow fences were erected at all the vulnerable spots north from Tyndrum. Having deteriorated through the middle years of the twentieth century, they have not been replaced.

While few winters would match the ferocity of 1894/5, few passed without incident and many were severe. That of 1962/3 proved so; and the new Type 2 Sulzers stood aside, while Black 5s returned to plough duty. The North British conceded that conditions on the West Highland were exceptional, not least during the months of winter, though insisting that 'south of Ardlui the men do not have the same claim'. It was recognised how 'married men stay better' – which implied a more generous provision of houses than first intended. Besides Fort William's Tweeddale Place (see Chapter Fifteen), a tenement was erected at Crianlarich. There were other considerations too – on a long and isolated single-track route, telegraph linesmen were needed close at hand to tend the tablet system. Homes along the line, when finally completed and in good order, were superior to the general run of late-nineteenth-century railwaymen's dwellings. The North British engineer thought them '£500 houses' (when his standard was £300), and he warned that he could not retain his surfacemen and permanent-way gangs if high rents were imposed. Rents were at first a general grievance, and the first tenants of Tweeddale Place petitioned (unsuccessfully) for a reduction, pleading the cost of living in Fort William. Stationmasters and signalmen at intermediate stations were expected to lodge their summer-relief colleagues.

A mail pouch from Bridge of Orchy, taken to and fro by goods train and entrusted to the Gorton signalman, gave the railway families of Strathtulla their postal service. From Ardlui northward several stations came to have post facilities and the stationmasters were appointed official sub-postmasters. Minor alterations to the station buildings were required, for which the North British, not untypically, expected the men to pay, out of their small GPO stipends, until a compromise was found. During the westward progress of the Callander & Oban in the 1860s and 1870s, the public gained access to the railway telegraph station by station. By the 1890s, the GPO wires had extended and the North British felt less need, along the West Highland, to be accommodating in the despatch or receipt of telegrams – though landowners exerted some pressure for a full service. Delivery over any distance was, of course, impractical.

Maintaining the West Highland was never to be an easy task. In the daily round over all the years of steam, the Fort William Ballast was as much a West Highland institution as the Sleeper or the Ghosts. It was stabled at the loading bank on the town-side of the old fort, in easy reach of the stores and workshops which occupied the ground later cleared for today's station, and comprised an old coach for the travelling squad, assorted wagons and a brake-van. Leaving early each morning, perhaps to join forces with its fellow from Crianlarich, the Ballast sauntered back in the late afternoon. (The engine might be turned at Rannoch but came home, as a rule, tender-first.) When the work in hand required, other wagons were attached at Mallaig Junction and shunted there on the return.

Snow clearing in the diesel era meant new expedients – for example, a Type 2 might propel an old tender, mounting a traditional plough. Practice has progressed, from independent snow ploughs to modern snow blowers. 'Care and repair' in general is today thoroughly mechanised and carefully programmed by NetworkRail. Alongside the economies achieved by radio-signalling and Sprinter operation, a realistic engineering budget keeps the West Highland viable. In this regard, the experimental 'Karrier' road-rail vehicle introduced by the LNER in the 1930s was certainly a portent.

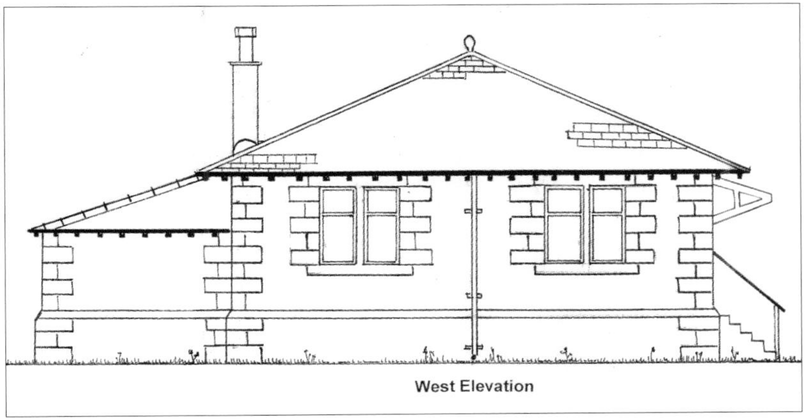

Stationmaster's house, Ardlui. (Futers)

Misfortune at Rannoch, January 1895. North British snow ploughs were adjusted by a hawser round the engine chimney – uncomfortably suggesting a hangman's noose (Hamilton-Ellis). Like others of their numerous class, the derailed 0-6-0s (then termed '18 inch Goods') would be rebuilt as Class C/J36. (Alsop)

Modern maintenance, Crianlarich viaduct. (Crawford)

Ballast working, near Cruach, in the 1940s, when snow fences were still kept in repair. The J36 has a tender-cab. (Stevenson)

Gorton under snow, looking south. (Stevenson)

Modern snow-blower, Crianlarich. (Crawford)

Cruach snow shed, looking south. (Crawford)

Tree clearing, Auchtertyre. The Friends of the West Highland Lines have pressed for traditional 'from the train' views to be recaptured. (McNab)

Chapter Twenty-Two

CLIMB TO CORROUR

West Highland trains in steam days might labour out of Queen Street, on the Cowlairs incline; but there was scope for relatively fast running onwards to Craigendoran. Thereafter (discounting the many minor peaks and troughs), the route presents three successive ascents, each summit higher than the last – from Garelochhead to Glen Douglas; from Ardlui to County March; and from Bridge of Orchy to Corrour. By contrast, the southbound journey begins with an ascent of 28 miles from sea level at Fort William to Corrour, broken only by the brief fall from Auchindaul into Spean Bridge. An engine starting 'cold' or steaming badly would struggle up Glen Spean and falter on the long gradient past Loch Treig. In 1937, on a windy summer day of sunshine and shower, O. S. Nock[1] recorded his definitive experience, when ex-North British *Glen Croe* and *Glen Loy* (LNER Nos 9406 and 9494) double-headed the afternoon Mallaig–Glasgow out of Fort William: with their 320-ton train they reached Corrour in sixty minutes, inclusive of three station stops, sustaining 26–29 mph against the gradients. Today's Sprinters are allowed fifty minutes, more or less.The route from Lochaber into Badenoch is age-old. The West Highland Railway takes this course through Spean Bridge and Roy Bridge, skirting the Ben Nevis range. At Tulloch, where the steep-sided, roadless valley of Loch Treig opens into Glen Spean, the line turns south for the heights of Rannoch.

1. Long-time contributor on locomotive performance to the *Railway Magazine* and other journals.

The Great Marquess starts confidently out of Tulloch and across Laggan viaduct with a seven-coach special (2012); in their heyday the K4s might take nine vehicles unaided. (Henshaw)

The *Royal Scotsman* on the Treig deviation. The original roadbed is exposed below. In the background the Spean–Laggan valley tends north-east to Badenoch and Strathspey. (Fielding)

66 737 heads an alumina 'empties' past Fersit. The grass-grown spoil heaps (left) date from the Lochaber power scheme. (Fielding)

In misty conditions, three decades earlier, a 'Black 5' slogs towards the plantation halfway up Loch Treig. (Stone)

Lightly loaded, 62005 turns inland at Lochtreighead. (Fielding)

With Loch Treig now hidden, the Up Sleeper follows Altachamabreac burn towards Lebruaridh. (Fielding)

Double-heading, 2-6-0 leads 4-4-0, *c.* 1930 – an Up passenger approaches Corrour distant signal. (Casserley)

62005 tops the summit. Corrour's original signal box-cum-cottage contrasts with the modern building, today an unlikely but popular restaurant. (Fielding)

The latest version (in both feet and metres) of the summit sign. (McNab)

Chapter Twenty-Three

A LANDOWNERS' LINE'?

The West Highland was presented, on the model of the Highland Railway and the Callander & Oban, as a bona fide local promotion in which landed proprietors, headed by Donald Cameron of Lochiel, 24th chief of Clan Cameron, had taken the lead. This disguised North British imperialism and softened the speculative interest of engineers Formans & McCall and contractors Lucas & Aird.

Along the route to Fort William, six major landlords held sway: Sir James Colquhoun of Luss, the Marquess of Breadalbane, Sir Robert Menzies of Weem, Colonel Gustavus Walker of Loch Treig, The Mackintosh and Lord Abinger. Lochiel's own lands were untouched, when the Glen Coe route was dropped, save for a small parcel on Rannoch Moor, but the Roshven extension, lost in Parliament, would have crossed his Fassifern estate. The Banavie branch required his consent and cooperation. Like Mrs Cameron-Campbell of Callart (see Chapter Fourteen), Lochiel benefited from new feuing in and around a growing Fort William once the West Highland opened. He stood to gain too from development at Onich (where he had already paid for a new pier), had the Fort William–North Ballachulish line been built.

The Colquhoun Trustees required that the railway be carried back from the shore along Loch Lomond, with an arched masonry viaduct at Craigenarden, the one exception to Charles Forman's standard girder spans. The alteration also produced the only tunnel on the West Highland as first built. Breadalbane's loyalties lay with the Highland Railway and the Callander & Oban, but he recognised a public interest and stood neutral, receiving £1,000 against the risk of damage to Blackmount Forest 'and disturbance of the deer therein' during construction, plus safeguards for his salmon pools on the River Orchy. Colonel Walker's initial objections disappeared when Sir John Stirling-Maxwell purchased Corrour Forest, the outlying portion of Loch Treig estate. The Mackintosh consented (but at a price) to the Glen Spean deviation through his Brae Lochaber property.

It is a question whether all the proprietors lived up to their pledges. On the other hand, the opportunity to take shares was restricted by the North British Company, intent that the West Highland be an obedient client. 'Native' members of the West Highland board were displaced by North British nominees. Lord Abinger, the first West Highland chairman (d. 1893), made way for the Marquess of

Tweeddale (see Chapter Eight). George Wieland, the North British secretary, doubled as secretary of the West Highland and became the key executive figure during construction. Of the original promoters, only Lochiel (d. 1905) and Captain (later Major) Roderick Colquhoun continued as West Highland directors.

Though the landowners' show of unity helped the West Highland Bill of 1888–9 through Parliament, their coalition was fragile. Sir Robert Menzies treated the road to Rannoch station as his own and attempted to restrict its use until the Perthshire local authorities intervened. The Mackintosh insisted that Inverlair station become 'Tulloch' (as it did from 1895) – Inverlair being, strictly speaking, across the River Spean on Lord Abinger's estate. Lochiel deprecated a 'quarrel about a sign board' but advised acquiescence – The Mackintosh's goodwill would be needed if a Laggan line were to be revived (see Chapter Eleven). The new Lord Abinger, seldom resident in Lochaber, refused to have an auction mart at Lochy Bridge (where Ben Nevis distillery siding might readily have been extended) and broke ranks by supporting the Invergarry & Fort Augustus Railway. He owned the hotel at Spean Bridge and thought a station at Gairlochy useful for his estate. Of a younger generation, Stirling-Maxwell was an enthusiast for conifer planting – he would head the post-1918 Forestry Commission. His paternalist concern for the families of successive signalmen at lonely Corrour is well recorded.

Landed influence in society (and in Parliament) long remained a given. The West Highland Company's proposed deviation on Rannoch Moor was refused, as likely to injure the Appin Trustees' deer sanctuary in the Black Corries west of Cruach, but the Glen Spean deviation, which cut the club-farms of The Mackintosh's tenants near Roy Bridge, was quickly approved.[1] The Marquess of Lorne, heir to the Duke of Argyll, declared with little finesse that the family might abandon Inveraray and the townspeople who depended on them for employment, if the Callander & Oban branch from Dalmally were to be built. They preferred the proposed light railway from West Highland Arrochar & Tarbet, which terminated on the opposite shore of Loch Fyne and would not invade the grounds of Inveraray castle (see Chapter Thirteen).

Breadalbane, with no thought of refusal, sought a brake-van pass for his marchioness, who used West Highland goods trains (paying first-class fares) on her expeditions from Forest Lodge (Blackmount). When the Crianlarich spur lay unused into 1897, Breadalbane castigated the North British for bad faith. In retaliation he threatened to oppose the treasury guarantee on which the Mallaig Extension depended and to support the Fort William commissioners in the foreshore quarrel there (see Chapter Fourteen). His tenants in Glen Falloch, Strathfillan and Glen Orchy urged Callander & Oban and West Highland to cooperate. Like the farmers of Loch Fyne (see Chapter Thirteen), they wanted rail access both south to Glasgow and east to Stirling and Perth.

Lord Burton, later to be the mainstay (at heavy cost) of the unfortunate Invergarry & Fort Augustus Railway, was the long-term lessee of Glen Quoich. (As Sir Michael Bass, brewer-MP, he had supported the Glasgow & North Western scheme.) In March of 1894, Burton was favoured with a journey over the unfinished West Highland line. He and his party, en route to Glen Quoich Lodge (via Spean Bridge), went from Craigendoran to Rannoch in contractor John Aird's inspection coach, changing there to a similar vehicle. (Charles Forman used the occasion to run a North British saloon through to Fort William for the first time, rousing excitement in Lochaber – a measure of the eagerness with which the new railway was awaited.) The expedition was subsequently described in a Burton-on-Trent newspaper: 'There is a long approach and a viaduct to finish at Rannoch and a bridge and approaches to construct at the River Gauer, which was in flood. A temporary line is laid at these points. It was very cold, all the small pools being quite frozen over and the ground covered with snow.'

The writer added that the navvies on Rannoch Moor, where the water was brackish, were supplied with Burton beer: 'Judging from the "empties" ready to be returned, this special permission has been fully appreciated.' The railway family at Gorton passing place would be supplied with water from the engine tenders when goods trains paused there.

Landlord influence notwithstanding, the crofter had found a political voice in the 1880s and depopulation was controversial. Earlier clearances came under scrutiny and the conversion of previously cleared land to sport – now that sheep farming had become less profitable – was inflammatory. The landlords had a case – a shooting and fishing estate provided more employment and generated more rail traffic, in and out of season, than untenanted sheep farms in the factor's hands – but it was a case difficult to sustain. In the promotion of the Mallaig Extension, landowners and Crofter-Liberal MPs made reluctant common cause. It was imperilled when Lord Abinger, as West Highland chairman, declared in an unguarded moment that his railway would serve the 'paying population', while hastening the 'surplus' on their way to Canada.

1. Historians gained, however: crofters' club-farms are not well documented and the railway plans have preserved a detailed record of the holdings at Achluachrach and Inverroy.

Donald Cameron of Lochiel, twenty-fourth chief of Clan Cameron, promoter and director of the West Highland Railway.

Landowners with shooting preserves along the West Highland line were promised 'grouse protectors' (on the telegraph wires) and deer fences. (*Mountain, Moor and Loch*)

New Inverlochy Castle, Torlundy, built in the 1860s – seat of Lord Abinger, promoter and first chairman of the West Highland Railway. The bare hillsides towards Auchindaul are today heavily forested. (Gillespie)

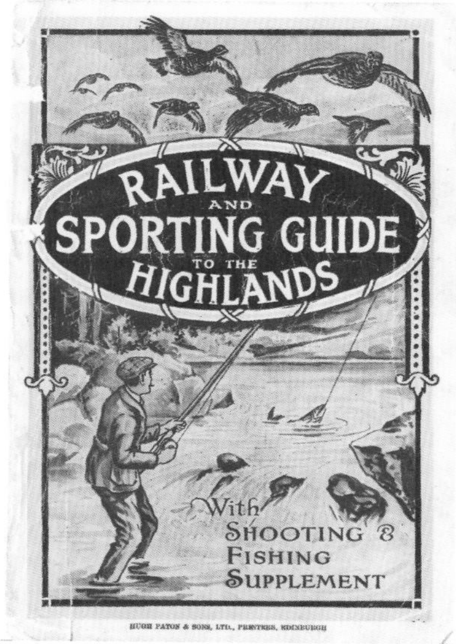

Seasonal 'sporting' traffic was important to every railway in the Highlands.

Chapter Twenty-Four

VIADUCTS

For many travellers, Charles Forman's shapely viaducts – masonry piers (some founded on concrete) and girder spans (predominantly of lattice form) – symbolise the West Highland line. Generations of photographers have discovered that many of them, bending with the railway, have a scenic location – the consequence of Forman's 'contouring' layout. Erection was economical, whenever possible. On the 'Horseshoe' at Auch, where the viaducts describe continuous curves, it was possible to dispense with conventional staging and run what was in effect a 'train' of girders on to the piers. The handsome masonry structure at Craigenarden, on Lochlomondside, is the exception: Forman proposed to hug the shore, causewaying the line at Inveruglas bay, but the Colquhoun Trustees required a higher, less obtrusive alignment and a traditional arched viaduct.

Craigenarden. (McNab)

Glen Falloch. (Henshaw)

Fillan Water. (Fielding)

Auchtertyre. (Henshaw)

Right: Achallader. (Henshaw)

Below left: Laggan (Tulloch). (Henshaw)

Below right: River Spean. (Fielding)

Southbound special, 'Horseshoe' 5-span viaduct. (Henshaw)

Auch Glen, 'Horseshoe' 8-span viaduct. (Fielding)

The Horseshoe Bend from Ben Dorain. (Stevenson)

Chapter Twenty-Five

DOUBLE-HEADING

When the West Highland Railway opened in 1894, the Board of Trade imposed a limit of 25 mph average speed, gradually relaxed over the next decade as numerous curves were eased and the track generally re-fettled. Ultimately, the 120 miles between Glasgow and Fort William could be covered in something over four hours, with station stops, including time to take water. That the diesel-hauled summer 'extras' of the mid-1960s were allowed exactly four hours was advertised as a leap forward. There might be brief sprints, which identified the more exuberant drivers (say, from Corrour downhill to Lochtreighead, northbound), or spells of relatively fast running (e.g. southbound, down Strathtulla), while a good overall pace could be sustained across Rannoch Moor, but time-keeping on the West Highland depended on a relatively fast and uncluttered run along the Clyde and, even more, on maintaining best speed uphill.

The North British Company's 'West Highland Bogie' 4-4-0 locomotives first put on passenger duty were sluggish climbers, soon found to require pilot assistance on trains exceeding four passenger coaches (the load for which they had been designed). Their *Glen* class successors, new in 1914 (and latterly LNER/BR Class D34), could take 180 tons unaided. The K2 Class 2-6-0 Lochs introduced in the 1920s by the LNER (not all were named) improved on this figure by 40 tons, while the three-cylinder K4 2-6-0s – six were built specifically for West Highland service from 1937 – at once showed themselves capable of handling nine coaches, some 300 tons. Unrivalled for sustained output on successive ascents, the K4s were nevertheless stressed at timetable speed between Glasgow and Craigendoran, and the 1950s saw them largely confined to the Mallaig Extension. During the final twenty years of steam, general workhorses of simple and robust construction prevailed – the BR K1 2-6-0 (derived from the K4s), and the latecoming 4-6-0 type (ex-LNER B1s, ex-LMS Black Fives and BR Standard 5s).

A pair of West Highland Bogies was a familiar sight in the line's earliest period – but so, in the middle years, was a pair of *Glens* or a pair of *Lochs* and, in later years, a pair of Black 5s. The heaviest trains were routinely double-headed and the introduction of successively more powerful locomotive classes did not end the practice. In the North British canon, perpetuated by the LNER and British Railways, the train engine led and the assisting engine was coupled 'inside' – as is obvious in the photographic record when different classes are represented. In that record over the decades are West Highland Bogies leading 0-6-0s, K2 *Lochs* leading D34 *Glens* and every permutation of 4-6-0 leading 2-6-0 (the K4s apart). Banking was all but unknown: assisting engines ran the entire route.

In the 1960s and 1970s Type 2 BRCW Sulzers (Class 27) were paired, as, from the 1980s, were the Type 3 EEs (Class 37). A 37 with an ETHEL 'inside' (see p.81 right) curiously suggested traditional practice. With the *Jacobite* firmly established as a summer feature on the Mallaig Extension, steam locomotives have returned to the West Highland proper, taking the coaches north at the beginning of the season and south at its end, and these workings have become advertised, well-patronised specials. Steam-worked charter trains also feature. Double-heading, if not always strictly necessary, is often operationally convenient – to the joy of enthusiasts and photographers. Steam paired with diesel (deliberately or to remedy a mishap) can also be experienced, and the relaxation of weight and other restrictions has brought several strangers, both steam and diesel, to Fort William (see Chapter Twenty-Seven).

Leaving Ardlui, two K2s tackle Glen Falloch. The leading engine is 61794 *Loch Oich*. (C. Lawson Kerr Collection, courtesy Stevenson)

A heavy southbound passenger tops County March. 'Black 5' and K2 pilot ('inside') was a regular pairing of the 1950s, especially on the winter-timetable Sleeper. (Yuill)

'B1 plus K2' on the approach to Fort William. (Yuill)

62005 (as 62012) and restored B1 61243 *Sir Harold Mitchell* approach County March from the north – six coaches are not a testing load. In the foreground, the old parliamentary road is now part of the West Highland Way. (Henshaw)

Glen Falloch almost mastered – K1 62005, in 'unhistorical' LNER green as 2005, leads 'Black 5' 44767 *George Stephenson.* (Henshaw)

2011: past the Gauer viaduct, *The Great Marquess* and *The Sherwood Forester* head the Scottish Railway Preservation Society's *West Highlander*. Since the 1960s Gorton to Rannoch, once the emptiest stretch of Rannoch Moor, has been invaded by modern forestry. (Gray)

11 August 1994, on the Treig deviation, 37 221 and 37 152 head the Centenary Special. Mark 1 coaches are in Intercity 'raspberry ripple' livery. (Henshaw)

7 August 1994 – public traffic on the West Highland began four days before the official opening, and a steam special marked *that* centenary, with '2005' and *The Great Marquess* in charge. The two 2-6-0s are seen at Fort William's Tomnafaire depot. (Henshaw)

Chapter Twenty-Six

ENGINES AND ENGINEMEN

Deep in discussion, Garelochhead. (Stevenson)

Oban trains at Arrochar & Tarbet, their regular morning 'meet' from 1966. With tablet hoop over his shoulder, the Glasgow Eastfield driver prepares to change over. (Stevenson)

Glen Falloch viaduct – from the cab of *The Great Marquess*. (Henshaw)

The line ahead, near Gorton – from the cab of 'Black 5' 44975. (Stone)

Chapter Twenty-Seven

VISITORS

4-6-0 essay – an LNER, ex-Great Eastern Railway, B12 at Crianlarich in 1938, heading green-and-cream excursion stock. For the summer service between Glasgow Queen Street and Oban, a B12, piloted by the only 'West Highland Bogie' to be rebuilt (becoming LNER Class D36 2695), satisfied Callander & Oban weight restrictions. (Yuill)

Unusual pilot – at Craigendoran Junction *c.* 1955, an ex-LNER 'Scottish Director' 4-4-0 (of Great Central Railway ancestry) is coupled inside 'Black 5' 45714 on a Down West Highland passenger. The extensive sidings were a relic of wartime traffic to and from Faslane. (C. Lawson Kerr, courtesy SRPS)

Clan Cameron at Ardlui in June 1956, bound for Spean Bridge and Cameron of Lochiel's seat at Achnacarry. (Stevenson)

Restored veterans – the unique Caledonian Railway 4-2-2 123 and North British 4-4-0 256 *Glen Douglas* at Ardlui in 1961. (Hamilton, courtesy MacDonald)

'K4 Farewell', June 1960 – pausing at Rannoch, *Cameron of Lochiel* is the centre of attention; the Renton Boulder commemorates the financier whose 'bridging loan' saw the West Highland to completion. (Casserley)

Southbound 'Harry Potter Train', with ex-Great Western Railway 4-6-0 5972, approaches Rannoch in 2009. The *Harry Potter* films featuring Glenfinnan viaduct on the Mallaig Extension have brought more visitors to Glenfinnan Station Museum. (Mathieson)

'Blue Pullman' at Fort William. (Carmichael)

Deputising for a '66', restored BR 'Deltic' 55 022 *Royal Scots Grey* heads alumina 'empties' near Auchindaul in May 2011. (Henshaw)

2008: *The Great Marquess* leads BR/ex-LMS Class 8F 48151 across Rannoch viaduct. (McNab)

Restored BRCW 'narrow' 33 207 *Jim Martin* heads the *Royal Scotsman* at Fort William. Motive power can vary but the luxury tour train is a familiar sight on the West Highland today. (Henshaw)

Chapter Twenty-Eight

PERIOD PIECES

The North British Company tenements at Fort William (named 'Tweeddale Place' for the chairman's lady), half-hidden by the heather arch celebrating Edward VII's visit in 1907. A similar arch graced the West Highland's opening day (see Chapter 8).

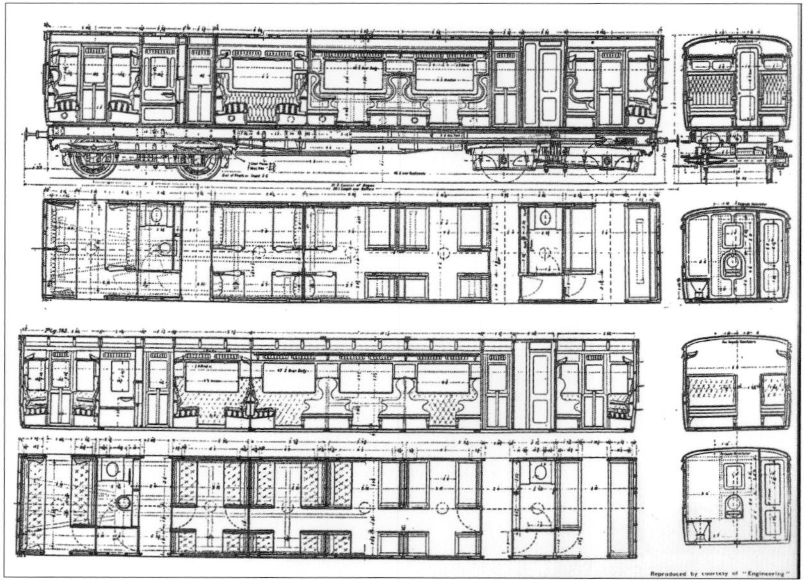

Compartment-and-saloon West Highland coaching stock, 1894. The first-class vehicles (upper drawings) were more generously proportioned.

NBR Class M 0-4-4T 239 on a local train at 'Upper Helensburgh'. The LNER preferred 'Helensburgh Upper' and the station has so remained, but lost its passing loop in the 1960s. (Alsop)

Fort William station frontage just after nationalisation, still in late LNER guise, with inevitable MacBrayne buses. (Robert Grieves Collection, courtesy Sinclair)

LNER V4 2-6-2 1700 *Bantam Cock* heads a Down goods of the 1940s in Glen Falloch, with wartime 'N.E.' lettering still in evidence. 1700 and nameless 1701 (unofficially *Bantam Hen*) were prototypes of a might-have-been mixed-traffic class. (Stevenson)

Leaving the Highlands behind, *c.* 1955 a 'Black 5' heads an Up passenger along the Gare Loch, above Faslane: the haycocks are 'period' too. (Yuill)

Fort William in BR days kept an ex-LMS 'Midland' 0-6-0 for snowplough duty. 44275 rests in Nevis distillery sidings, along with a variety of wagons, cattle trucks and a horsebox. (Stone)

At Fort William signalbox, the fireman of BR K1/1 61997 *MacCailin Mor* receives the tablet for the short section past the old fort yard and over the River Nevis to Mallaig Junction. One of six K4s, *MacCailin Mor* was rebuilt as the K1 prototype. (Yuill)

The Gorton signalman halts a Down passenger for two members of a railway family travelling to Fort William, *c.* 1960. The old coach was once a school room for the railwaymen's children of Gorton and Strathtulla: a 'lady teacher' travelled from Bridge of Orchy. (SRPS)

Tokens exchanged at Spean Bridge *c.* 1970: operation by single-line tablet continued until the 1980s. (Stevenson)

Transition – a BRCW Sulzer partners a 'Black 5' on an Up passenger above Loch Treig. (Stone)

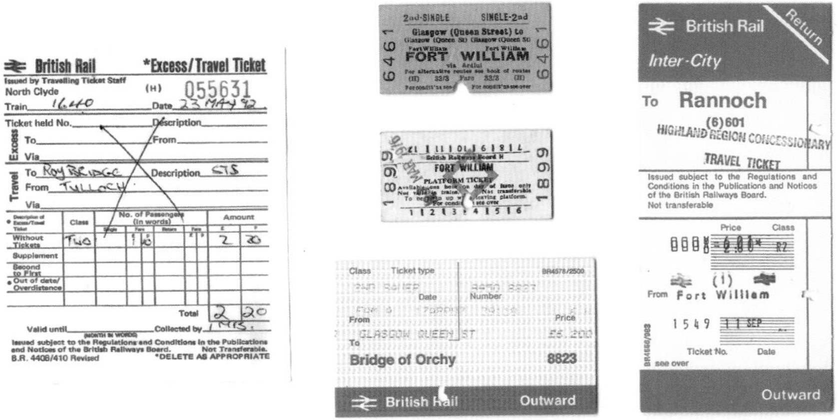

Tickets – evolution. Platform tickets at Fort William's new station (1975) were a short-lived innovation.

'Westie' logo.

Chapter Twenty-Nine

LEISURE

The opponents of the West Highland attacked first Roshven and then Mallaig as unsuitable harbours, adding that, in any case, the promoters had exaggerated the potential of the west coast fishery. The treasury would be embarrassed, they predicted, to have guaranteed a railway with tourists as its principal business…

This was hyperbole; but tourist traffic loomed large from the outset on the West Highland proper. The compartment-and-saloon coaches specially built by the North British Company had been designed with the views in mind (though the original picture-windows were soon modified to improve ventilation). On-train information helped travellers trace the route and the guide book *Mountain, Moor and Loch* was pleasingly illustrated. The artist had sketched his way to Lochaber during the final months of construction, wandering among the navvies and riding on ballast trains. He bore the not infrequent rain cheerfully, only complaining that his favourite 'London tobacco' was nowhere obtainable. Besides lauding the scenery, the text recounted Highland legends and tapped the works of Sir Walter Scott and Robert Louis Stevenson.

While a range of day excursions was programmed, summer traffic in the period on to 1914 was still very much of the 'extended tour' variety for the middle-class and upper-class market, in cooperation with other railway companies and with David MacBrayne. Several of these circular expeditions included the all-day passage of the Caledonian Canal from Banavie to Inverness or vice versa. Though allocating spartan rolling stock to the short journey between Fort William and Banavie Pier, the North British were keenly aware that many summer travellers on the canal were 'first class and cabin' (as against 'third class and steerage'). A mass market was beginning to develop, and the Polytechnic Touring Association, looking to successive day trips from a single centre over the course of a week or fortnight, saw Fort William as a possible base. Nevertheless, in the summers prior to the First World War the North British found it sufficient to run 'extras' on the Mallaig line just three days a week.

The fashionable Highland season, August–October, meant not just across-the-Border first-class return traffic but toing and froing by rail within Scotland as house parties moved about; moreover, accompanying servants, 'indoor' and 'outdoor', luggage and other equipment generated additional revenue at third-class rates. The Invergarry & Fort Augustus promoters made much of the sporting estates in (or within reach) of the Great Glen. However, the Fort Augustus line, and the West Highland too, were latecomers to this table. As elsewhere in the Highlands, horse-and-carriage business – traditionally a year-round standby which expanded markedly in summer and autumn – began to decline when the well-to-do discovered that the convenience of motoring might outweigh its hazards. Patronage of Shandon Hydropathic fell away too as fashions changed (see Chapter Seventeen).

Though the 1930s Depression trapped a sizeable minority, in broad terms the years between the wars saw improved living standards and more widespread paid holidays, with corresponding changes in leisure patterns. The LNER introduced camping coaches at a number of West Highland locations and (experimentally) converted two stations on the Invergarry & Fort Augustus (with no passenger service from 1933) to holiday apartments. New excursion stock – open, not compartment (which gave more window seats), in cheerful green-and-cream – came into summer service on the West Highland, on which day-trip business markedly increased. Sunday excursions from Glasgow to Fort William were indicative of changing mores – Sabbatarianism was on the wane. The Northern Belle hotel train 'cruised' the LNER's more scenic lines every summer from 1933, and the seven-day programme regularly included the West Highland: in a typical itinerary the voyagers took a Loch Lomond steamer to Ardlui, whence the *Belle*'s day coaches ran to Mallaig and back to Fort William, where the night coaches now waited. Meanwhile, older tourist traditions were dwindling. Summer sailings on the Caledonian Canal ended in 1939.

The Austerity years post-1945 saw summer traffic recover slowly to a mid-1950s peak. June–September provision on the Mallaig Extension reached its maximum while weekend services between Glasgow and Fort William (at the beginning and end of a holiday week or fortnight) were strengthened and duplicated. MacBrayne's summer programme, with connecting trains and motor-coaches, returned to 1930s proportions. Camping coaches were reintroduced. An enterprising innovation from 1956 was the introduction of observation cars on the Callander & Oban, Dingwall & Skye and West Highland lines. One of the ex-LNER 'Coronation' vehicles was allocated to the Mallaig Extension and ultimately made the round trip twice daily; the other ran from Glasgow to Fort William on the mid-morning service, returning south each evening.

From around 1960 road improvements, expanding car-ownership and the increasing possibilities of foreign travel spelled a long retreat from rail travel. The perception gained ground that the railways of the western Highlands were ultimately doomed – an outlook which made every attempt to revive tourist use seem half-hearted. Confidence has been regained in some measure since the 1980s, thanks to the steam-hauled *Jacobite*, to wider 'railway heritage' traffic and to the buoyant outdoor activities market – exemplified in the conversion of Bridge of Orchy station building to a walkers' bunkhouse and the extension of the building at Tulloch into a hostel. The well-established West Highland Way, incorporating parts of the old parliamentary road over Blackmount and terminating at Fort William, is readily accessed at Ardlui, Crianlarich, Tyndrum and Bridge of Orchy, and additional long-distance footpaths are being developed. Skiing and mountain biking at Nevis Range (Aonach Mor) near Torlundy have brought year-round traffic.

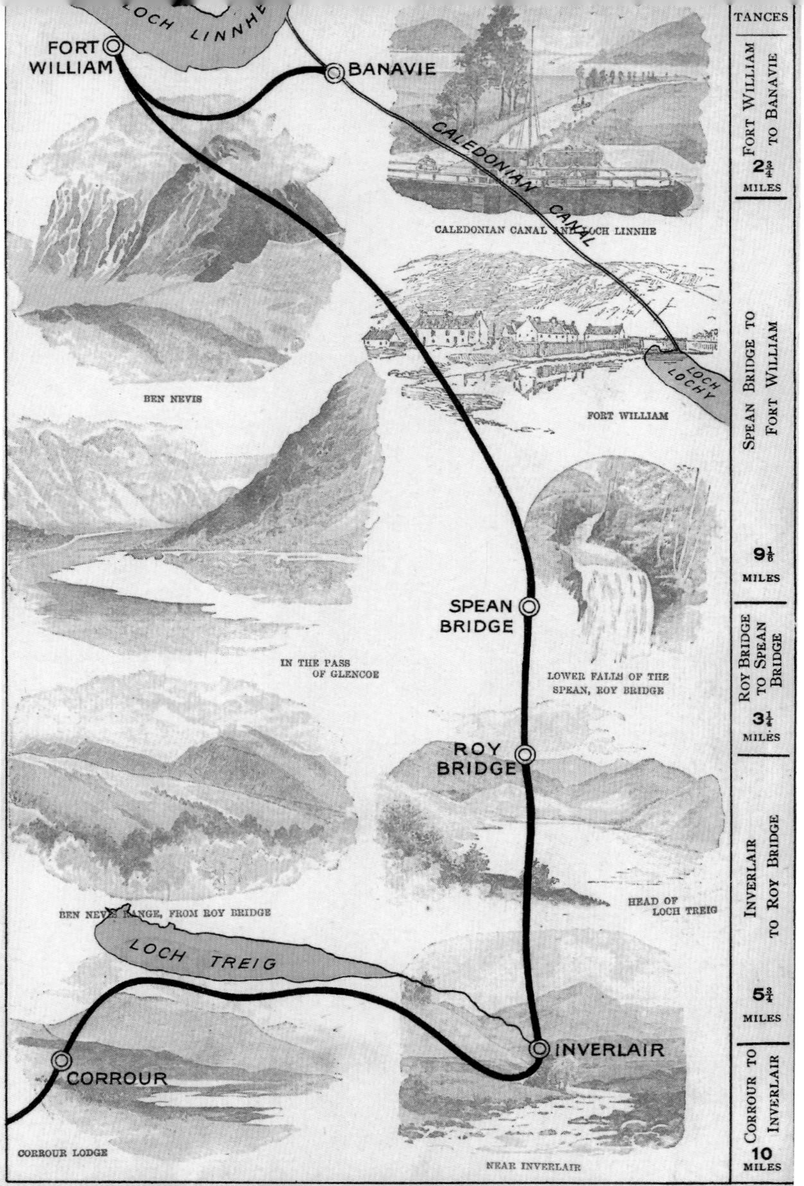

CORROUR TO FORT WILLIAM AND BANAVIE.

TOUR No. 26–c.

BRIDGE OF ORCHY, GLENCOE, BALLACHULISH, FORT-WILLIAM, OBAN, AND CRINAN.

TRAIN, COACH, AND STEAMBOAT HOURS.

Going to Fort-William via Bridge of Orchy and Ballachulish, returning via Oban and Crinan Canal.

			a.m.	a.m.	
	Edinburgh (Waverley)	depart	6 25	...	...
	Do. (Haymarket)	,,	6 29	......	......
	Glasgow (Queen Street High Level)	,,	7 30	...	...
	Bridge of Orchy	arrive	10 12	......	......
Coach	Do.	depart	10 15	...	...
Coach	Ballachulish	arrive	4 15	......	......
Steamer	Do.	depart	6 45	...	...
Steamer	Fort-William	arrive	7 40	......	......
Steamer	Do.	depart	p.m.	5 10	...
	Glasgow (Queen Street Low Level)	arrive	......	6 3	......
	Edinburgh (Waverley)	,,	...	7 10	...

Going to Fort-William via Crinan Canal and Oban, returning via Ballachulish and Bridge of Orchy.

			a.m.	a.m.	
	Edinburgh (Waverley)	depart	7 20	...	...
	Do. (Haymarket)	,,	7 24	......	......
	Glasgow (Queen Street Low Level)	,,	8 2	...	...
	Fort-William	arrive	7 40	......	......
Steamer	Do.	depart	p.m.	9 20	...
Steamer	Ballachulish...	arrive	......	10 20	......
Coach	Do.	depart	...	12 0	...
Coach	Bridge of Orchy	arrive	......	5 45	......
	Do.	depart	...	6 23	...
	Glasgow (Queen Street High Level)	arrive	......	9 8	......
	Edinburgh (Waverley)	,,	...	10 23	...

FARES, including Coachman's Fees.

	1st Cl. & Cabin. s. d.	3rd Cl. & Steerage. s. d.
Edinburgh (Waverley and Haymarket ...	48 8	34 1
Glasgow (Queen Street) ...	41 2	30 1

Tickets valid during the Season, and Passengers may break the journey at any place on the Route. The Route may be reversed.

One of several extended circular tours offered by the North British Company in association with David MacBrayne. The coach link between Bridge of Orchy and Ballachulish took the then parliamentary road by Inveroran, Kingshouse and Glencoe – a route nowadays familiar to walkers on the West Highland Way.

Traveller's linear map: final page, Corrour–Banavie. (*Mountain, Moor and Loch*)

Callander station, depicted in the first official West Highland guide. Day tours embracing the Trossachs and Loch Lomond, utilising both the Callander & Oban line and the West Highland, continued into BR days. (*Mountain, Moor and Loch*)

Shandon Hydropathic. (McCutcheon)

1930s: the *Northern Belle* at Fort William. 9035 *Glen Gloy* leads. (The *Belle*'s day and night portions were both allocated a pair of 'Glens'). (P. Woods)

1930s: camping coach, Crianlarich, where shunting trains entertained the 'campers'. The engine is K2 4697 *Loch Quoich*. (Stevenson)

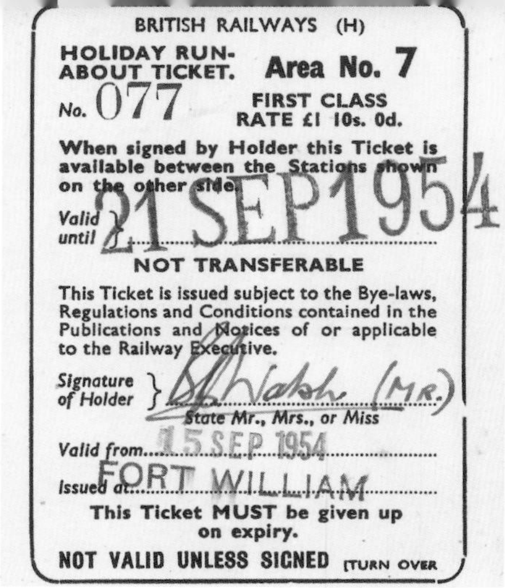
BRITISH RAILWAYS (H)

HOLIDAY RUN-ABOUT TICKET. **Area No. 7**

No. 077 FIRST CLASS RATE £1 10s. 0d.

When signed by Holder this Ticket is available between the Stations shown on the other side.

Valid until 21 SEP 1954

NOT TRANSFERABLE

This Ticket is issued subject to the Bye-laws, Regulations and Conditions contained in the Publications and Notices of or applicable to the Railway Executive.

Signature of Holder (MR.)

State Mr., Mrs., or Miss

Valid from 15 SEP 1954

Issued at FORT WILLIAM

This Ticket MUST be given up on expiry.

NOT VALID UNLESS SIGNED [TURN OVER

BR's Callander & Oban-cum-West Highland Runabout Ticket for a week's unlimited travel. Poor connections at Crianlarich made careful planning imperative. With a relatively lavish summer service on the Extension, the cheaper Roy Bridge-Fort William-Mallaig Runabout was the more popular. (SRPS)

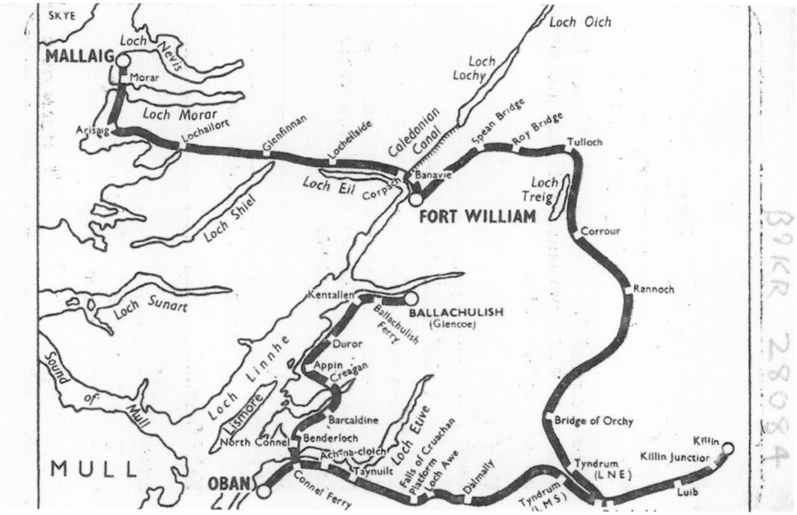

BR observation car programme, *c.* 1960.

SEE SCOTLAND THE "RAIL" WAY

Travel in the OBSERVATION CARS operating MONDAYS to SATURDAYS on the following routes:-

GLASGOW and OBAN

4th May to 19th September

		am			pm
GLASGOW (Buchanan Street)	dep	7 55	OBAN	dep	5 30
		pm			
OBAN	arr	12 28	GLASGOW (Buchanan Street)	arr	9 25

Supplementary fare for the single journey in either direction

3/6

Accommodation can be reserved in advance on application to the Reservation Office, Glasgow (Buchanan Street) (for journeys commencing from Glasgow) and to the Station Master, Oban (for journeys commencing from Oban), on payment of the supplementary fare.

GLASGOW and FORT WILLIAM

13th June to 5th September

		am			pm
GLASGOW (Queen Street)	dep	10 5	FORT WILLIAM	dep	5 10
		pm			
FORT WILLIAM	arr	2 5	GLASGOW (Queen Street)	arr	9 10

Supplementary fare for the single journey in either direction

3/6

Accommodation can be reserved in advance on application to the Reservation Office, Glasgow (Queen Street) (for journeys commencing from Glasgow) and to the Station Master, Fort William (for journeys commencing from Fort William), on payment of the supplementary fare.

FORT WILLIAM and MALLAIG

		B	A	C			C	D
		am	am	pm			pm	pm
FORT WILLIAM	dep	9 55	10 30	2 45	MALLAIG	dep	12 30	5 42
			noon					
MALLAIG	arr	11 30	12 0	4 27	FORT WILLIAM	arr	1 52	7 18

A—4th to 30th May and from 28th September to 10th October **B**—1st June to 26th September
C—15th June to 5th September **D**—4th May to 26th September

Supplementary fare for the single journey in either direction

2/6

Accommodation can be reserved in advance on application to the Station Master, Fort William (for journeys commencing from Fort William) and to the Station Master, Mallaig (for journeys commencing from Mallaig), on payment of the supplementary fare.

INVERNESS and KYLE OF LOCHALSH

		E	F			G
		am	am			pm
INVERNESS	dep	10 40	9 25	KYLE OF LOCHALSH	dep	5 30
		pm	pm			
KYLE OF LOCHALSH	arr	1 40	12 20	INVERNESS	arr	8 30

E—4th May to 26th June and from 7th to 28th September. **F**—27th June to 5th September
G—4th May to 28th September

Supplementary fare for the single journey in either direction

3/6

Accommodation can be reserved in advance on application to the Station Master, Inverness (for journeys commencing from Inverness) and to the Station Master, Kyle of Lochalsh (for journeys commencing from Kyle of Lochalsh), on payment of the supplementary fare.

61997
OBSERVATION CAR

A 'Coronation' car, its original 'beaver tail' modified, on the turntable at Fort William. (Glenfinnan Station Museum Trust)

Tulloch station building – now a hostel for climbers, bikers and walkers. (Furnevel)

INTERCITY
Luxury
Land Cruises
&
Luxury
Days Out
Winter 1993/4
8 October 1993 to 23 May 1994

Intercity Land Cruise programme, 1990s.

Chapter Thirty

STEAMERS

North British Railway paddle steamers at Craigendoran. Tourist programmes *c.* 1900 offered Clyde Coast excursions from as far away as Dundee, Fort William or Galashiels. (McCutcheon)

MacBrayne's *Gondolier*, from Inverness bound for Banavie, enters Fort Augustus 'stair' on the Caledonian Canal. In the right background is the Invergarry & Fort Augustus viaduct over the River Oich. (John Penny Collection, courtesy Carmichael)

MacBrayne's *King George V* approaches Fort William *c.* 1950. The prominent notice warned engine drivers to proceed at walking pace when their trains invaded the pierhead. (Robert Grieves Collection, courtesy Sinclair)

David MacBrayne (1818–1907), founder of the celebrated western Highlands and Islands shipping company, which later expanded into passenger buses and road haulage.

Chapter Thirty-One

STEAM RESTORED

2008: Standard 4 2-6-0 76001, having served a season on the *Jacobite*, pilots Black 5 45407 *The Lancashire Fusilier* south from Ardlui. BR 2-6-0s had a brief innings on the Mallaig Extension in the 1950s. (Henshaw)

The Great Marquess in the heart of Glen Falloch, heading the 'West Highlander' (2009). (McNab)

2012: a '37', 62005 and support coach, en route to Fort William, emerge from Cruach snow shed. (Fielding)

Black 5s 44871 and *The Lancashire Fusilier* in tandem, climbing towards Corrour, work their end-of-season passage south on a SRPS special (October 2012). (Gray)

62005 takes a five-coach Down special past Loch-na-Chlaidheimh. (Henshaw)

Supposed LNER 2005 in Monessie Gorge, where ancient rocks hem in the River Spean. (Henshaw)

Chapter Thirty-Two

OLD FORT AND TOMNAFAIRE

Fort William shed in the 1930s, when 2-6-0s and 4-4-0s had pride of place. The nearer engines are 9035 *Glen Gloy* and 4685 *Loch Treig*. (McCutcheon)

Shunting the yard, 1950s: 65313 has the morning duty. A 'Black 5' rests just within the shed. (Stevenson)

Tomnafaire: '37s' in strength and evidence of timber traffic, with Lochy viaduct in the left background. (Henshaw)

The Great Marquess, *Lord of the Isles* (so-called) and *The Sherwood Forester*. Behind is Tomnafaire hill (seen from the opposite side in p.76 right). (Henshaw)

Right: Tomnafaire: 62005 returns by road after firebox repairs (September 2013). (Henshaw)

Chapter Thirty-Three

ENVOIE

The Fort Augustus line was closed completely in 1947, the Banavie branch in 1951. In other respects, change came slowly to the ex-North British, ex-LNER, West Highland route in the first dozen years of state ownership. LMS standardisation had already crept over both the Callander & Oban route and the entire system of the former Highland Railway. The Beeching Report (1962) was chilling, the ensuing reprieve a huge relief, when the Wiggins-Teape pulp and paper mill to be established at Annat was heralded as the West Highland's saviour. On the face of things, and very much contrary to the general tide of closures across Scotland, the future looked relatively secure – though traditional fish traffic was lost to road transport (1965) and passenger figures continued to edge downwards.

The Arrochar & Tarbet shuttle ended (1964). Craigendoran (West Highland), Rhu, Shandon and Whitlefield disappeared; Helensburgh Upper and Roy Bridge lost their passing loops. Nevertheless the increase in traffic was manifest. Where the evening journey north from Glasgow in the winter months had entailed a single 'meet', there were now successive crossings. The surviving Oban service contributed three additional passenger trains in each direction south of Crianlarich (see Chapter Sixteen) Besides china clay and chemicals north and finished paper south, workings for the Annat mill included a daily timber train. Loading at Crianlarich's abandoned Callander & Oban station, it reversed to use the Crianlarich spur, reversed once more to face Fort William and reversed a third time at Mallaig Junction. Tyndrum, Bridge of Orchy and Gorton took on an up-to-date appearance, re-signalled for optional looping.

The West Highland's reprieve had another dimension, better appreciated now that the Cold War had receded, in that the upper reaches of Loch Linnhe between the Corran Narrows and Fort William were judged to possess Defence potential, as a reserve base supplementary to the latest installations in the sea lochs opening from the Clyde estuary. After 1945, 'secret' Faslane had become a ship-breaking yard, thus continuing to generate rail traffic. It now became the Royal Navy's controversial Polaris submarine depot, with a supporting facility at Glen Douglas, where the security lighting, chain fence and partially concealed bunkers seemed ominously forbidding. Nature would soften this sombre scene, but occasional Ministry of Defence freight workings still catch the attention of the passing traveller. Faslane, now the Navy's Trident submarine base, is no longer rail-connected.

That the longer term was after all uncertain became the key note of the 1970s and 1980s. Livestock traffic had gone. Oil traffic might follow. Though goods, transmogrified into block freight workings, retained some importance, it was at the mercy of remote 'strategic decisions'. Wood-pulping at Annat had proved commercially unviable. A niche market continued for certain papers, with pulp brought north by rail, but this makeshift contradicted all the earlier projections. It was uneasily reminiscent of the North British Company's experience after 1901, when the hopes invested in fish traffic were found to be unrealistic.

Even in high summer, passenger business dwindled. In the new order post-Beeching, a buffet-restaurant car (from Glasgow to Mallaig and back) still complemented the sleeper, while the morning Mallaig–Glasgow attached a buffet car at Fort William, to return on the evening Glasgow–Mallaig. (During the morning and evening 'meets' the buffet-restaurant staff passed a cooked meal to their lone colleague in the other train – a discreet window-to-window operation at side-platform Spean Bridge but a public performance at island-platform Crianlarich.) As on other lines in the Highlands, these vehicles had civilised what were often protracted journeys. While the economic arguments may have been unanswerable, the withdrawal of these vehicles was, for many, confirmation of a sad downward path. Meanwhile, BR Mark 2 coaches largely replaced the Mark 1 vehicles dating from around 1950. Trains were shorter – in part because high-capacity open stock became the second-class standard. Open coaches two-thirds empty sent a pessimistic message – and the improvised miniature buffets imparted little cheer.

Today, all activity at Annat has finally ceased and the Oban line no longer feeds freight of any sort to the southern half of the West Highland. A continuing traffic in timber, oil and aluminium slab has been precariously stop/go. Alumina is still carried to Fort William – in bulk, twice a week, from Blythe, south of the Border – but it might be brought more readily by sea. (Curiously, this had been North British Aluminium's original intention, before reaching agreement with the LNER.)

On balance, however, these negatives are offset by the positives of more recent decades. Leisure travel has revived (see Chapter Twenty-nine). The establishment of Glenfinnan Station Museum in 1991, a declaration of faith that the West Highland would endure, has become an attraction in its own right. Whatever the implications for employment along the route, RETB has reduced operating costs. Despite the Sprinters' limitations, they have helped make possible year-round a timetable more generous than ever before, with three services on weekdays in each direction between Glasgow and Mallaig and Sunday provision, which began tentatively in the final years of locomotive haulage, now matter-of-fact. Above all, the re-introducton of steam on the Mallaig Extension (1984) has gone from strength to strength summer by summer, with obvious benefits for the West Highland proper.

Inter-company rivalries, politico-economic ideologies and pusillanimous Governments prevented the achievement of an integrated railway system for northern Scotland in the latter part of the nineteenth century. But it is some compensation that the West Highland line and its Mallaig Extension stand largely intact in 2014.

Glen Dochart, looking west to Luib and Ben More. For almost half a century Oban trains have used the West Highland, while much of the Callander & Oban line, eastward from Crianlarich, has returned to nature. (Gray)

The RETB centre, Banavie, on the site of Banavie Canal Bridge signalbox, now controls the entire West Highland system – and the swing bridge. (Johnstone)

Invergarry station, under restoration, will become an information centre on the Great Glen footpath and cycle route. The subway entry has been rediscovered … (Gray)

RETB notice, Bridge of Orchy. Physical token has become radio message. The special seen in p.121 upper right approaches the level crossing on the sometime parliamentary road, now the West Highland Way. (Johnstone)

A Mallaig–Glasgow Sprinter at Upper Tyndrum, running traditionally 'left hand'. Under RETB, with spring-loaded points, 'left hand' or 'right hand' is dictated by siding layout. (Henshaw)

The Down Sleeper on Lochtreigside, where in June 2012 a landslide overwhelmed 66 734 and its loaded alumina tankers. The casualty (shrouded, bottom right) was eventually cut up on the spot. (Crawford)

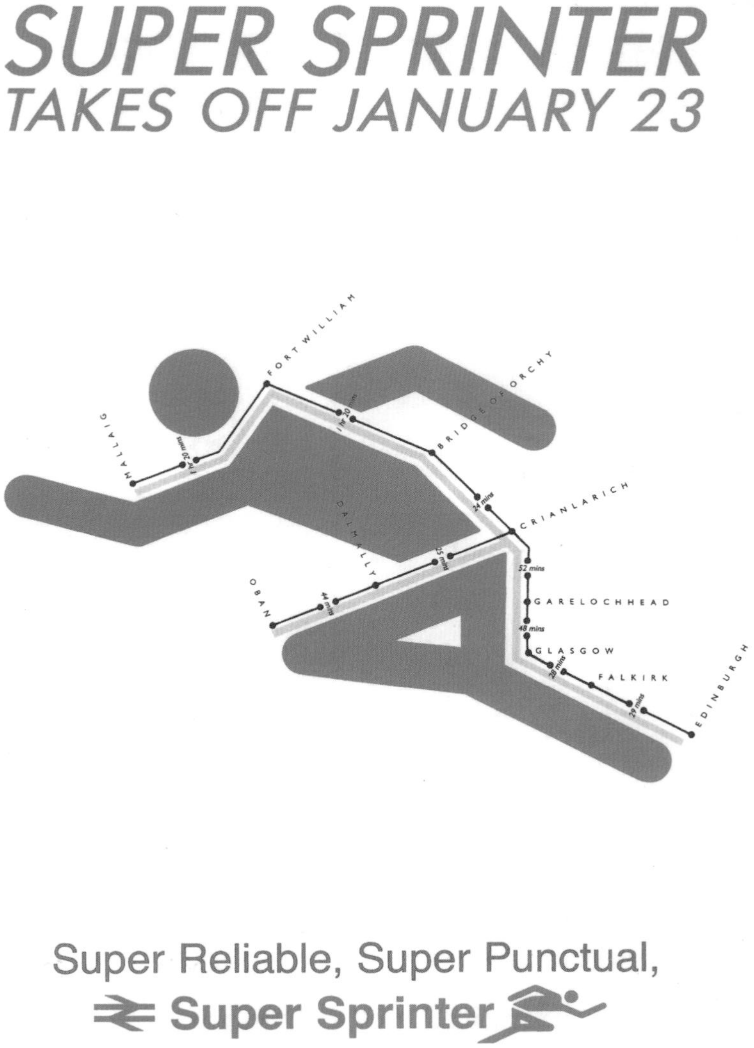

Sprinters coming – advance publicity, 1989.

Fort William's 'recycled' turntable is testimony to the success of restored steam. (Henshaw)

Vestigial freight – a lightly loaded '66', southbound, passes Roy Bridge, where the passing loop and Up side 'chalet' building are long gone. (Henshaw)